Not a Mystery

UNDERSTANDING GOD

Ken LeBrun

Prophecy Waymarks Publications
Helena, Montana

Because
that which may be known
of God is clearly seen,
even His eternal power
and Godhead; so that they
are without excuse.

Romans 1:19, 20

CONTENTS

INTRODUCTION

Let's begin with the obvious: There is a whole lot about God that we don't know. This book is not about those things. We'll leave them with God.

> The secret things belong unto the Lord our God: but those things which are revealed belong unto us and to our children for ever, that we may do all the words of this law. (Deuteronomy 29:29)

Jesus said, "Unto whomsoever much is given, of him shall be much required." Luke 12:48. So we see a correlation between what God has given and what He requires. He only requires of us the information about Himself that He has given. That's a relief! And the more important the truth, the more clearly He has revealed it.

We're going to focus in this book on what God has plainly told us about Himself. To venture beyond His explanations would be treacherous and pointless. Our thesis is twofold:

1. God has provided plenty of information for us to know Him.

2. The nature of that revelation, to the extent that it has been given, is accurate and clear.

> Those important matters that concern our salvation were *not left involved in mystery.* They were not revealed in such a way as to perplex and mislead the honest seeker after truth. Said the Lord by the prophet Habakkuk: "Write the vision, and make it *plain,...* that he may run that readeth it." Habakkuk 2:2. The word of God is *plain* to all who

study it with a prayerful heart.[1]

The essential doctrines of the faith are presented in the Bible in a *clear* and *simple* manner, so that all men may understand them.[2]

The great truths which concern our redemption are *clearly* presented.[3]

In discussions about the Trinity it is common for people to get so tangled up that they toss up their hands and say, "It's a mystery! We can't understand it."

Well, I have good news. God, in His word, has already provided all the answers we need. And His explanations are *clear.*

The Scriptures *clearly* indicate the relation between God and Christ, and they bring to view as clearly the personality and individuality of each.[4]

So, instead of trying to force an interpretation onto the sacred text, we just need to notice what the Bible *plainly* and *clearly* says. This doesn't need to be hard.

---

1   Ellen G. White, *The Great Controversy*, p. 521. Unless otherwise noted, emphasis in all quotations is supplied.

2   *Ibid.*, p. 243.

3   *Ibid.*, p. 526.

4   White, *Testimonies for the Church*, Vol. 8, p. 268.

INITIAL INVESTIGATION

No belief is more fundamental than the one that identifies the God we worship. The current Seventh-day Adventist understanding of God is summarized in our second Fundamental Belief.

> There is one God: Father, Son, and Holy Spirit, a unity of three coeternal Persons. God is immortal, all-powerful, all-knowing, above all, and ever present. He is infinite and beyond human comprehension, yet known through His self-revelation. God, who is love, is forever worthy of worship, adoration, and service by the whole creation. (Gen. 1:26; Deut. 6:4; Isa. 6:8; Matt. 28:19; John 3:16; 2 Cor. 1:21, 22; 13:14; Eph. 4:4–6; 1 Peter 1:2.)

This belief statement may be broken down into three components:

1. A *declaration* of one God
2. A *definition* of the one God
3. A *description* of the one God

The *declaration* simply says, "There is one God." The *definition* of that one God is "Father, Son, and Holy Spirit, a unity of three coeternal Persons." And the *description* of the one God takes up the remainder of the statement. Finally, to this statement is attached nine Bible references to provide a scriptural basis. We assume these texts would have been selected for their clarity in expressing the Bible's teaching on this subject. The three elements in our statement should be easily found in the verses selected. If not there, we'll find them *somewhere* in God's word, because that's just what He has promised.

So, we're going to briefly examine each of the listed Bible references, specifically looking for a *declaration* of one God, a *definition* of the one God, and a *description* of the one God that matches our doctrinal statement. At the end of the chapter we will summarize the data.

Genesis 1:26

> And God said, Let us make man in our image, after our likeness: and let them have dominion over the fish of the sea, and over the fowl of the air, and over the cattle, and over all the earth, and over every creeping thing that creepeth upon the earth.

This verse contributes to our *description* of God as "above all" and "worthy of worship, adoration, and service by the whole creation." The fact that God created man and gave him dominion over all the earth demonstrates God's supremacy over all.

The verse does not explicitly *declare* that there is one God, so we will wait to find that *declaration* elsewhere.

What about our *definition* of the one God? Does this verse help us here? The *definition* we are looking for is something equivalent to "Father, Son, and Holy Spirit, a unity of three coeternal Persons."

It is often pointed out that the Hebrew word for God in this verse, *elohim*, is plural in form, a fact that may suggest a plurality of persons within the definition of the one God. God's statement, "Let *us* make man in *our* image," adds support to this thought.

The argument, however, is not conclusive. The Jews, from whose body of literature Genesis comes, and whose native tongue was Hebrew, did not consider God to be a plurality of persons as is now taught, but rather a single Being. Their knowledge of the Hebrew language provided allowance for a suffix that normally denotes plurality, to be attached to the title of their singular God. Jacques Doukhan explains that "the use of the plural form of the word *Elohim* expresses the idea of majesty and transcendence."[5] It does not require God to be plural in person. We find the same "plural of majesty" applied in 1 Kings 11:33 to "Ashtoreth the goddess (*elohim*) of the Zidonians, Chemosh the god (*elohim*) of the Moabites, and Milcom the god (*elohim*) of the children of Ammon." These are single gods, each one individually designated as an *elohim*. Clearly, the plural form of this word does not demand a numerically plural application.

This is reinforced by the use of the singular verb "said" in Genesis 1:26. If more than one person was speaking, the Hebrew verb would naturally be plural in form. But the Hebrew form of the verb in this sentence is third person singular, indicating a single speaker. The next verse continues in the same way, "So God created [singular verb] man in his [singular pronoun] own image, in the image of God created he [singular verb] him; male and female created he [singular verb] them."

We have no need for uncertainty on this point. We know exactly who was speaking to whom in this case:

> And now God said to His Son, "Let us make man in our image."[6]

It was a single speaker, addressing a single listener. God was speaking to His Son. If we impose upon the text our definition of God as a unity of three Persons, it becomes confusing. But with the natural reading it all makes sense. The Father was

---

5   *Genesis*, Adult Sabbath School Bible Study Guide, General Conference of Seventh-day Adventists, April/May/June 2022, p. 7.
6   White, *The Story of Redemption*, pp. 20, 21.

speaking to His Son.

This understanding of *elohim* is affirmed in Daniel 3:25 where Nebuchadnezzar exclaims, "Lo, I see four men loose, walking in the midst of the fire, and they have no hurt; and the form of the fourth is like the Son of God."[7] The word for "God" here is *elahin*, the Aramaic equivalent of the Hebrew *elohim*. In spite of having a plural form, this is a clear reference to God the Father, for the One in the flames was identified as His Son. This is He whom Jesus called "my Father" nearly sixty times in the New Testament.

So we see that the plural suffix on the word *elohim* does not, in itself, clearly indicate that God is a plurality of Persons.

Let's look at the second verse cited.

Deuteronomy 6:4

> Hear, O Israel: The Lord our God is one Lord.

As a *description* of the one God, this verse contributes little. In terms of a *declaration* of one God, it is more to the point. Traditionally observant Jews recite this *Shema* twice a day in affirmation of God's singularity. English translations vary, but oneness is the main concept conveyed in each of them.

It is usually pointed out that the Hebrew word for "one" here is *echad*, a word that can be used for one group, such as one cluster of grapes. It is used in Genesis 2:24 of the oneness of Adam and Eve, two people who were "one flesh." This observation, however, still does not prove God to be a plurality. In Genesis 2:21, God took "one" (*echad*) of Adam's ribs to form Eve. We understand this to mean a single rib. *Echad* does not require an interpretation that inherently denotes a group. Consider Deuteronomy 17:6 where the testimony of two or three

---

7   "And in the form of the fourth in the midst of the fire the king recognized the Son of God." White, *Prophets and Kings*, p. 509.

witnesses could condemn a man to death, but with only one (*echad*) witness, he would not die. In this example, *echad* cannot mean two or three.

Glyn Parfitt has compiled a full list of all the Old Testament verses in which he feels *echad* could mean "united in one."[8] He has assigned that meaning to the word 43 times in 36 Old Testament verses. That sounds pretty good until we realize that *echad* is used 951 times in 739 verses. So according to Parfitt's analysis *echad* carries the meaning of "united in one" less than five percent of the time. The word simply means "one." Just as in English we may apply the word "one" either to a single item or to a single group of items, so it is with the Hebrew *echad*. The word itself does not indicate plurality.

So, while Deuteronomy 6:4 is a good *declaration* of one God, it does not provide the *definition* of the one God that we are looking for.

Isaiah 6:8

> Also I heard the voice of the Lord, saying, Whom shall I send, and who will go for us? Then said I, Here am I; send me.

No *declaration* of "one God" is found here. The comment in our statement's *description* of God that He is "known through His self-revelation" is supported in this verse in that the Lord is calling a prophet to represent Him and speak on His behalf. But what about our *definition* of the one God as a unity of three Persons? The rationale for the selection of this verse most likely had to do with its use of the word "us." This word could give evidence of a plural Lord speaking. Or, it could simply be the same situation that we found in Genesis 1:26—the

---

8   Glyn Parfitt, *The Trinity: What Has God Revealed? Objections Answered*, pp. 665, 666.

Lord addressing some other heavenly being. The fact that He says, "Whom shall I send," seems to indicate a singular speaker. There is nothing in the verse that urges us to reject the natural reading—i.e., that one Individual is speaking to another.

Matthew 28:19

> Go ye therefore, and teach all nations, baptizing them in the name of the Father, and of the Son, and of the Holy Ghost.

This verse gives no *declaration* of one God. Nor does it provide any *description* of our one God. It is included as a supporting scripture because it specifically speaks of the Father, the Son, and the Holy Spirit.

Have we now found our *definition* of the one God as a unity of three Persons? We've clearly found the three Persons, but what about our definition? If this verse *is* a definition, it unfortunately doesn't tell us what it's defining. To say that Jesus is here providing a definition of "one God" is to go beyond what He actually said. We're looking for a clear and unmistakable definition of that expression.

What this verse does tell us is that there is a Father, a Son, and a Holy Ghost. This revelation is valuable in light of verse 20 where Jesus specifies what we are to teach—"all things whatsoever I have commanded you." Christ's simple explanations—from His own mouth and also through His prophets—are to provide the content of our teaching. We have no other commission.

John 3:16

> For God so loved the world, that he gave his only begotten Son, that whosoever believeth in him should not perish, but have everlasting life.

This verse contains no outright *declaration* of one God; it seems to be understood and therefore unnecessary to be said. The use of the definite article before the word "God" [*ò theós*] suggests that there is only one. The verbs "loved" and "gave" are expressed in the third person singular, consistent with the singular subject.

Our *description* of the one God, "who is love," is illustrated in this verse, revealing the extent of His love for us.

Our *definition* of the "one God" as "Father, Son, and Holy Spirit" doesn't really work with this verse. The designation "God" here clearly indicates the Father, because we know that "the Father sent the Son to be the Saviour of the world." 1 John 4:14.

2 Corinthians 1:21, 22

> Now he which stablisheth us with you in Christ, and hath anointed us, is God; who hath also sealed us, and given the earnest of the Spirit in our hearts.

Here we find "Christ" and "God" and "the Spirit," who are referred to by Ellen White as "the eternal heavenly dignitaries."[9] The reference to "God" in this case is again to the Father. It is He, Paul tells us, "which stablisheth us with you in Christ, and hath anointed us." And it is He "who hath also sealed us, and given the earnest of the Spirit in our hearts."

This centrality of the Father in the plan of redemption is brought out again in Chapter 5 of the same epistle:

> And all things are of God, who hath reconciled us to himself by Jesus Christ, and hath given to us the ministry of reconciliation; to wit, that God was in Christ, reconciling the world unto himself, not imputing their trespasses unto them; and hath committed unto us the word of reconcil-

---

9   White, *Evangelism*, p. 616.

iation…. We pray you in Christ's stead, be ye reconciled to God. For he hath made him to be sin for us, who knew no sin; that we might be made the righteousness of God in him. (2 Corinthians 5:18-21)

Second Corinthians 1:21, 22 does not offer a *definition* of "one God." However, as already mentioned, the title "God," as used here, does appear to refer to the Father. This does not deny the divinity of Christ and the Holy Spirit, but our present quest is for a clear biblical definition of the expression "one God." If it's an essential point, it will be clear.

This passage makes no overt *declaration* of one God, nor is our *description* of the one God found in it.

2 Corinthians 13:14

The grace of the Lord Jesus Christ, and the love of God, and the communion of the Holy Ghost, be with you all. Amen.

In this verse we again find "Jesus Christ" and "God" and "the Holy Ghost." The designation "God" in this context still clearly refers to the Father. A *definition* of the "one God" that embraces all three Persons is still missing.

Nor does this verse present a clear *declaration* of one God. But its reference to "the love of God" does support our *description* of the one God, "who is love."

Ephesians 4:4-6

There is one body, and one Spirit, even as ye are called in one hope of your calling; one Lord, one faith, one baptism, one God and Father of all, who is above all, and through all, and in you all.

We have finally discovered a New Testament passage with a clear *declaration* of "one God." And with it we find our first clear *definition* of the "one God." The "one God" is here defined as the "Father," who is clearly distinguished from the "one Spirit" and the "one Lord," the latter indicating Jesus Christ. Thus the "three highest powers in heaven"[10] are differentiated. But this biblical *definition* of the one God does differ from the one advanced in Fundamental Belief #2.

Our *description* of the one God as being "above all" comes directly from this passage. And our statement of Him being "ever present" is consistent with this verse's affirmation that God is "in you all."

1 Peter 1:2

> Elect according to the foreknowledge of God the Father, through sanctification of the Spirit, unto obedience and sprinkling of the blood of Jesus Christ: Grace unto you, and peace, be multiplied.

Once again we have God the Father, the Spirit, and Jesus Christ. With no *declaration* of "one God," the verse does not present itself as a *definition* of that expression. But it does speak of "God" specifically in reference to the Father.

As for a *description* of the one God, this verse's mention of His foreknowledge supports our statement of Him being all-knowing.

Analyzing the Data

So, there we have them—the verses presenting the Bible's best expression of the doctrine of the Trinity. How well did they do? Let's take a look at the results, beginning with the *description* component of our statement.

---

10   *Ibid.,* p. 617.

DESCRIPTION OF THE "ONE GOD"

	Genesis 1:26	Deuteronomy 6:4	Isaiah 6:8	Matthew 28:19	John 3:16	2 Corinthians 1:21, 22	2 Corinthians 13:14	Ephesians 4:4-6	1 Peter 1:2
IMMORTAL	○	○	○	○	○	○	○	○	○
ALL-POWERFUL	○	○	○	○	○	○	○	○	○
ALL-KNOWING	○	○	○	○	○	○	○	○	●
ABOVE ALL	●	○	○	○	○	○	○	●	○
EVER PRESENT	○	○	○	○	○	○	○	●	○
INFINITE	○	○	○	○	○	○	○	○	○
INCOMPREHENSIBLE	○	○	○	○	○	○	○	○	○
SELF-REVEALING	○	○	●	○	○	○	○	○	○
LOVE	○	○	○	○	●	○	●	○	○
WORTHY OF WORSHIP	●	○	○	○	○	○	○	○	○
WORTHY OF SERVICE	●	○	○	○	○	○	○	○	○

As we can see from the chart, these verses don't cover all the bases. There are, however, a few scattered hits. We'll just say that if a verse addressed *one* of the listed attributes of God, the *description* component was present. Now we need to add in the other two components.

THE "ONE GOD" IN FB#2

	Genesis 1:26	Deuteronomy 6:4	Isaiah 6:8	Matthew 28:19	John 3:16	2 Corinthians 1:21, 22	2 Corinthians 13:14	Ephesians 4:4-6	1 Peter 1:2
DECLARATION	○	●	○	○	○	○	○	●	○
DEFINITION	○	○	○	○	○	○	○	▧	○
DESCRIPTION	●	○	●	○	●	○	●	●	●

● Component present
○ Component missing
▧ Contrary to expectations

Only two texts in our list contain a *declaration* of "one God," and only one of them actually *defines* the expression. The *definition* it offers, however, is different from the one set forth in our Fundamental Belief statement. And as we saw in the first table, four of the eleven characteristics in our *description* of God are not brought out at all in the selected verses.

But that's fine because, true to the nature of God's self-revelation, the Bible does, in other verses, provide a direct *declaration* of one God, a straightforward *definition* of the one God, and a clear *description* of God. Notice the clarity of these texts:

A Declaration of "One God"

And the scribe said unto him, Well, Master, thou hast said the truth: for *there is one God*; and there is none other but he. (Mark 12:32)

As concerning therefore the eating of those things that are offered in sacrifice unto idols, we know that an idol is nothing in the world, and that *there is none other God but one*. (1 Corinthians 8:4)

For *there is one God*, and one mediator between God and men, the man Christ Jesus. (1 Timothy 2:5)

Thou believest that *there is one God*; thou doest well: the devils also believe, and tremble. (James 2:19)

A Definition of the "One God"

But to us there is but one God, *the Father*, of whom are all things, and we in him; and one Lord Jesus Christ, by whom are all things, and we by him. (1 Corinthians 8:6)

One God and *Father* of all, who is above all, and through all, and in you all. (Ephesians 4:6)

These words spake Jesus, and lifted up his eyes to heaven, and said, Father, the hour is come; glorify thy Son, that thy Son also may glorify thee:... And this is life eternal, that they might know *thee the only true God*, and Jesus Christ, whom thou hast sent. (John 17:1, 3)

A Description of the One God

Immortal: 1 Timothy 1:17; 6:16
All-powerful: Jeremiah 32:17; Luke 1:37
All-knowing: 1 John 3:20

Above all: Psalm 103:19
Ever present: Psalm 46:1; 139:7–10
Infinite: Psalm 147:5
Beyond human comprehension: Job 11:7; Romans 11:33
Known through His self-revelation: Numbers 12:6; Hebrews 1:1–3
Love: 1 John 4:8, 16
Worthy of worship and adoration: Psalm 18:3; Revelation 4:11
Worthy of service: Joshua 24:14-24; 1 John 4:19

Summary of our Assessment

The weakest component in Fundamental Belief #2 is our *definition* of the "one God." Of the nine Bible references listed, none were found to supply our voted definition. We learned that the Bible actually defines God in a simpler way than does our statement of belief. That's the beauty of divine revelation. In keeping with God's desire for us to truly know and understand Him, His Word is plain and clear to all who will simply receive it.

ALL TRUTH

In this chapter we're going to address two questions. We'll take them one at a time.

1. In the history of the Christian church, did the rise of the famous ecumenical councils represent an advancement in the understanding of truth, or an apostasy from it?

To help us with the answer, let's go back to the upper room in Jerusalem, A.D. 31. In Jesus' last instruction to His disciples before His crucifixion, He said, "I have yet many things to say unto you, but ye cannot bear them now. Howbeit when he, the Spirit of truth, is come, he will guide you into all truth." John 16:12, 13.

Into *how much* truth would the Holy Spirit guide the church? Jesus said clearly, "all truth."

And *when* exactly would that happen? Jesus promised it would be "when he, the Spirit of truth, is come." Christ was here referring to the outpouring of the Holy Spirit. That happened on the day of Pentecost. When the Holy Spirit was poured out, He would guide the church into *all* truth.

> In Christ's day many heard the gospel, but their minds were darkened by false teaching, and they did not recognize in the humble Teacher of Galilee the Sent of God. But after Christ's ascension His enthronement in His mediatorial kingdom was signalized by the outpouring of the Holy Spirit. On the day of Pentecost the Spirit was given.

Christ's witnesses proclaimed the power of a risen Saviour. *The light of heaven penetrated the darkened minds of those who had been deceived* by the enemies of Christ. They now saw Him exalted to be "a Prince and a Saviour, for to give repentance to Israel, and forgiveness of sins." Acts 5:31. They saw Him encircled with the glory of heaven, with infinite treasures in His hands to bestow upon all who would turn from their rebellion. As the apostles set forth the glory of the Only-Begotten of the Father, three thousand souls were convicted.[11]

Every principle of truth was given to the church from the very outset. The earliest Christians understood the Sabbath truth (Acts 16:13), the non-immortality of the soul (Acts 2:29, 34), the immutability of God's law (Acts 21:20; 22:12), salvation though Christ alone (Acts 4:12) to be received by faith and repentance (Acts 20:21), the divinity and personality of the Holy Spirit (Acts 5:3, 4), the second coming of Christ (Acts 1:11) and the resurrection of the dead, both for the just and for the unjust (Acts 24:15). They even understood that God had already set the date for the judgment (Acts 17:31), and that when the times of refreshing shall come, the sins of God's people will at that time be blotted out (Acts 3:19).

What about their understanding of God?

> But this I confess unto thee, that after the way which they call heresy, so worship I the God of my fathers, believing all things which are written in the law and in the prophets. (Acts 24:14)

Paul worshipped his fathers' God. "The God of Abraham, and of Isaac, and of Jacob, the God of our fathers," Peter declared, "hath glorified his Son Jesus," and "hath raised [him] from the dead." Acts 3:13, 15. The God of their fathers, having

---

11   White, *Christ's Object Lessons*, pp. 119, 120.

glorified His Son Jesus, was clearly God the Father. Paul explained it this way:

> But to us there is but one God, the Father, of whom are all things, and we in him; and one Lord Jesus Christ, by whom are all things, and we by him. (1 Corinthians 8:6)

> For there is one God, and one mediator between God and men, the man Christ Jesus. (1 Timothy 2:5)

The apostles' primary message was about Jesus. As soon as Paul was baptized, "straightway he preached Christ in the synagogues, that he is the Son of God." Acts 9:20. And the very last record of Paul in the book of Acts finds him still "teaching those things which concern the Lord Jesus Christ, with all confidence, no man forbidding him." Acts 28:31.

How thoroughly did Paul instruct his converts? "*I kept back nothing* that was profitable unto you, but have shewed you, and have taught you publickly, and from house to house." Acts 20:20. "For I have not shunned to declare unto you *all the counsel of God*." Acts 20:27. To the early church was declared all the counsel of God. "And so were the churches established in the faith." Acts 16:5.

What we never find Paul teaching is the doctrine of the Trinity. Neither he nor any of the other apostles ever defined God as a unity of three Persons. The Trinitarian definition of God was not established as a Christian doctrine until the year 381.[12] That's a full 350 years after the church was imbued with the Spirit of truth, whom Jesus said would guide her into all truth.

---

12   "The Church had to wait for more than three hundred years for a final synthesis, for not until the council of Constantinople (381) was the formula of one God existing in three co-eternal Persons formally ratified." –J. N. D. Kelly, *Early Christian Doctrines* (London: Adam & Charles Black), fourth ed., 1968, pp. 87, 88.

Did it take a third of a millennium, an edict of the emperor, and the raucous clamor of haughty bishops in ecumenical council, to finally bring about the fulfillment of Jesus' promise that the church would learn all truth? If it did, then Jesus missed the mark when He said, "When he, the Spirit of truth, is come, he will guide you into all truth." For it was not when the Spirit came that the church developed the concept of a triune God.

Did the early church advance in truth, or drift from it? Paul anticipated a crisis for which he "ceased not to warn every one night and day with tears." "After my departing," he warned, "shall grievous wolves enter in among you, not sparing the flock. Also of your own selves shall men arise, speaking perverse things, to draw away disciples after them." Acts 20:29-31.

Peter gave the same warning:

> There shall be false teachers among you, who privily shall bring in damnable heresies.... And many shall follow their pernicious ways; by reason of whom the way of truth shall be evil spoken of. (2 Peter 2:1, 2)

Jude noted,

> Beloved, when I gave all diligence to write unto you of the common salvation, it was needful for me to write unto you, and exhort you that ye should earnestly contend for the faith which was once delivered unto the saints. For there are certain men crept in unawares, who were before of old ordained to this condemnation, ungodly men, turning the grace of our God into lasciviousness, and denying the only Lord God, and our Lord Jesus Christ. (Jude 3, 4)

The unmistakable prediction of the apostles was that into the church would creep false doctrines. Instead of developing further into truth, the church would apostatize from it. "The day of Christ...shall not come, except there come a falling away first." 2 Thessalonians 2:2, 3. And history has proven their prediction to be correct. "It was apostasy," says Ellen White, "that led the early church to seek the aid of the civil government, and this prepared the way for the development of the papacy—the beast."[13] The church did not grow into truth, but in fact fell away from it.

> During and after Constantine's reign the church...became involved in a succession of doctrinal controversies that resulted in the crystallization of dogma, frequently along lines supported better by tradition and by pagan philosophy and practice than by Scripture, and thus Christianity became a creedal system. The church had achieved seeming success in the sight of men, but it had already apostatized in the sight of God.[14]

> These apostate Christians, uniting with their half-pagan companions, directed their warfare against the most essential features of the doctrines of Christ.[15]

> When the early church became corrupted by departing from the simplicity of the gospel and accepting heathen rites and customs, she lost the Spirit and power of God; and in order to control the consciences of the people, she sought the support of the secular power. The result was the papacy, a church that controlled the power of the state and employed it to further her own ends, especially for the punishment of "heresy."[16]

There it says clearly, "she lost the Spirit and power of God." It would be unreasonable to assume that for as long as she was under the control of the promised Spirit of truth, the early

---

13 *The Great Controversy*, p. 443.
14 F. D. Nichol, editor, *Seventh-day Adventist Bible Commentary*, Vol. 7, 1957, p. 20.
15 *The Story of Redemption,* p. 324.
16 *The Great Controversy*, p. 443.

church misunderstood some essential element of truth, which she did not get right for hundreds of years until she had "lost the Spirit and power of God."

The tumultuous attempts of the Roman church to define orthodoxy line up squarely with the predicted falling away from the purity of the faith which was once delivered unto the saints.

My second question is like the first, only this time we'll look at Seventh-day Adventist history:

2. Was the Seventh-day Adventist Church doctrinally correct from the time it was organized, or have the theological developments since that time been a necessary correction?

The great apostasy foretold in Scripture was not permitted to obscure the truth forever. In the eighth chapter of Daniel we find the story of the little horn power that would "cast down the truth to the ground." Daniel 8:12. There the question is asked, "How long shall be the vision concerning the daily sacrifice, and the transgression of desolation, to give both the sanctuary and the host to be trodden under foot?" Daniel 8:13. And the answer is given, "Unto two thousand and three hundred days; then shall the sanctuary be cleansed." Daniel 8:14. In context, this verse was predicting that 1844 would bring an answer to the desolation created by the little horn. In fulfillment of this prophecy, God in 1844 raised up a people to whom He restored the truth of the Sabbath, the soon coming of Jesus, the non-immortality of the soul, the appointed time of the judgment, and every other doctrine that had been buried beneath human tradition. The truth was no longer cast down.

> Many of our people do not realize how firmly the foundation of our faith has been laid. My husband, Elder Joseph Bates, Father Pierce, Elder Edson, and others who were keen, noble, and true, were among those who, after the

passing of time in 1844, searched for the truth as for hidden treasure. I met with them, and we studied and prayed earnestly. Often we remained together until late at night, and sometimes through the entire night, praying for light and studying the Word. Again and again these brethren came together to study the Bible, in order that they might know its meaning, and be prepared to teach it with power. When they came to the point in their study where they said, "We can do nothing more," the Spirit of the Lord would come upon me, I would be taken off in vision, and a clear explanation of the passages we had been studying would be given me, with instruction as to how we were to labor and teach effectively. Thus light was given that helped us to understand the scriptures in regard to Christ, His mission, and His priesthood. A line of truth extending from that time to the time when we shall enter the city of God, was made plain to me, and I gave to others the instruction that the Lord had given me.[17]

Notice that God gave those pioneers light specifically "to understand the scriptures in regard to Christ." "A line of truth," she says, "was made *plain* to me." The clear light given to the church at that time in regard to Christ was to shine until "the time when we shall enter the city of God."

We do not realize, says the prophet, "how firmly the foundation of our faith was laid." What is the foundation of our faith? "For other foundation can no man lay than that is laid, which is Jesus Christ." 1 Corinthians 3:11. When Peter confessed to Jesus, "Thou art the Christ, the Son of the living God," "Peter had expressed the truth which is the foundation of the church's faith."[18]

As Ellen White describes how firmly the foundation was laid, she says in the next paragraph, "All the principle points

---

17   White, *Selected Messages*, Book One, pp. 206, 207.

18   White, *The Desire of Ages*, p. 413.

of our faith were made clear to our minds, in harmony with the Word of God."[19] Just as Jesus had promised all truth to the first generation of Christians, so "*all* the principle points of our faith" were made clear to the minds of the first generation of Seventh-day Adventists.

By 1850 Ellen White could announce, "We have the truth. We know it. Praise the Lord."[20]

In 1869 she wrote, "We have no doubt, neither have we had a doubt for years, that the doctrines we hold today are present truth."[21]

In 1872 those doctrines were spelled out in a document entitled, *A Declaration of the Fundamental Principles Taught and Practiced by the Seventh-day Adventists*. It was "a brief statement of what is, and has been, with great unanimity, held by them." That statement of beliefs, with very little alteration, continued to be circulated by the church throughout the rest of Ellen White's lifetime.

In 1873 she wrote, "As a people we are triumphing in the clearness and strength of the truth. We are fully sustained in our positions by an overwhelming amount of plain Scriptural testimony."[22]

In 1881 she declared, "It is as certain that we have the truth as that God lives."[23]

And in reference to how much light they enjoyed at that time, she said, "We have not given heed to fables, but to the 'sure word of prophecy.' We are now living in the full blaze of the light of Bible truth."[24]

Yet, just as in the apostolic church, that full blaze of light

---

19   *Selected Messages*, Book One, p. 207.
20   White, *Manuscript Releases*, Vol. 19, p. 128.
21   White, *Testimonies for the Church*, Vol. 2, p. 355.
22   *Ibid.*, Vol. 3, p. 253.
23   *Ibid.*, Vol. 4, p. 595.
24   *Ibid.*, p. 592.

did not include the doctrine of the Trinity. The *Declaration of Fundamental Principles*, held with great unanimity among our people, was "distinctly non-Trinitarian."[25] In fact, the definition of "one God" as a unity of three Persons was not officially adopted by Seventh-day Adventists until 1980. That was a hundred and thirty-six years after 1844.

Was Ellen White mistaken when she said that all the principle points of our faith were made clear to their minds in her day? Is not an understanding of God a principle point of our faith? Did the century that elapsed between enjoying "the full blaze of the light of Bible truth" and the final Friday-afternoon vote in Dallas, represent a period of advancing light, or of slipping from it?

What had the servant of the Lord predicted? The fact is that she voiced the very same warning the apostles had given:

> I tell you now, that when I am laid to rest, great changes will take place. I do not know when I shall be taken; and I desire to warn all against the devices of the devil. I want the people to know that I warned them fully before my death.[26]

Do we know what type of changes the Lord foresaw? Yes, we are told the following:

> I have been instructed to warn our people; for many are in danger of receiving theories and sophistries that undermine the foundation pillars of the faith.[27]

> Be not deceived; many will depart from the faith, giving heed to seducing spirits and doctrines of devils. We have now before us the alpha of this danger. The omega will

---

25   North American Division of Seventh-day Adventists, *Issues: The Seventh-day Adventist Church and Certain Private Ministries*, 1992, p. 39.

26   White, Ms1-1915, February 24, 1915.

27   *Selected Messages*, Book One, pp. 196, 197.

be of a *most startling* nature.[28]

In the book *Living Temple* there is presented the alpha of deadly heresies. The omega will follow, and will be received by those who are not willing to heed the warning God has given.[29]

Living Temple contains the alpha of these theories. I knew that the omega would follow in a little while; and I trembled for our people.[30]

The enemy of souls has sought to bring in the supposition that a great reformation was to take place among Seventh-day Adventists, and that this reformation would consist in giving up the doctrines which stand as the pillars of our faith, and engaging in a process of reorganization. Were this reformation to take place, what would result? The principles of truth that God in His wisdom has given to the remnant church, would be discarded. Our religion would be changed. *The fundamental principles that have sustained the work for the last fifty years would be accounted as error.* A new organization would be established. Books of a new order would be written. A system of intellectual philosophy would be introduced.[31]

Has this happened? How do we feel about the *Fundamental Principles* that sustained the work in those days? What about their definition of God? The *Declaration of Fundamental Principles* presented the "one God" as the Father:

> **I.** That there is one God, a personal, spiritual being, the Creator of all things, omnipotent, omniscient, and eternal, infinite in wisdom, holiness, justice, goodness, truth, and

---

28   *Ibid.*, p. 197.
29   *Ibid.*, p. 200.
30   *Ibid.*, p. 203.
31   *Ibid.*, p. 204.

mercy; unchangeable, and everywhere present by His representative, the Holy Spirit.

II. That there is one Lord Jesus Christ, the Son of the eternal Father, the One by whom God created all things, and by whom they do consist....

That statement, published in the *SDA Yearbook* through 1914, was prefaced with the observation that upon these points, "there is, so far as is known, entire unanimity throughout the body."

That simple understanding of "one God" was upheld by the prophet herself:

Let the missionaries of the cross proclaim that there is one God, and one Mediator between God and man, who is Jesus Christ the Son of the Infinite God. This needs to be proclaimed throughout every church in our land. Christians need to know this.[32]

They have one God and one Saviour; and one Spirit—the Spirit of Christ—is to bring unity into their ranks.[33]

"Adventist beliefs *have changed* over the years...," observed William Johnsson in 1994. "*Most startling* is the teaching regarding Jesus.... Likewise the Trinitarian understanding of God."[34]

So we return to our question. Have we advanced in the light, or have we departed from it? It must be one or the other, for our beliefs have changed.

As we think about what has happened, we remember Ellen White's 1901 prediction that "we may have to remain here in this world because of insubordination many more years."[35] Still

---

32   *The Ellen G. White 1888 Materials*, p. 886.
33   *Testimonies for the Church*, Vol. 9, p. 189.
34   William G. Johnsson, *Adventist Review*, January 6, 1994, p. 10.
35   *Evangelism*, p. 696.

here we are, long after we were told that Jesus might have come "ere this."[36] Something hasn't gone according to plan. Jesus has not yet come. In light of that sobering reality, we need to be honest with ourselves. Do we today, stalled under the curse of the delay, imagine that God has given a clearer revelation of Himself to us in our lukewarm condition, than He gave after the passing of time in 1844 to those "who were keen, noble, and true," when "a clear explanation of the passages" studied was given through a living prophet of God, to whom truth was "made *plain*," and "*all* the principle points of our faith were made *clear*" to their minds?

"In the early days of the Advent Movement," Ellen White says, "the truth…was wrought out amid demonstration of the Spirit and of power."[37]

I don't think we've seen that today. The indication is that we are not even as apt as our forefathers to discern truth. Referring to those who "*had an experience in the work from the very rise of the third angel's message,*"[38] Ellen White says,

> Those who, in their experience, have passed over the ground and acted a part in the proclamation of the first, second, and third angel's messages, *are not so liable to be led into false paths* as are those who have not had an experimental knowledge of the people of God.[39]

> Shall a new foundation be built up by men to whom God has not granted the special experience He has granted to the men whom He ordained to establish the foundations of our faith?[40]

---

36 *General Conference Bulletin*, April 4, 1901.
37 Arthur L. White, *Ellen G. White: Vol. 5—The Early Elmshaven Years: 1900-1905*, p. 421.
38 *Manuscript Releases*, Vol. 17, p. 3, par. 2.
39 *Ibid.*, p. 1, par. 7.
40 Ellen G. White, Letter 232, 1903, par. 45.

Speaking in 1896 of Brother John Bell, she says,

> If he had passed through the experience of God's people as He has led them for the last forty years, he would be *better prepared to make the correct application of Scripture.*[41]

In light of all we have seen, it would be a rather ill-considered conclusion to imagine we grasp the truth better than did those whom God called to pioneer this message—better, in fact, than did the apostles themselves! When we learn that both the early New Testament church and the early Seventh-day Adventist Church were blessed with a comprehension of *all* the principle points of faith, along with warnings against an inevitable departure from that faith, we do well to seriously question the introduction of any new doctrine.

---

41   *Manuscript Releases*, Vol. 17, p. 1, par. 5.

"Every plant, which my heavenly Father hath
not planted, shall be rooted up."

Matthew 15:13

PREACH THE WORD

"In the golden censer of truth, as presented in Christ's teachings, we have that which will convict and convert souls. Present, in the simplicity of Christ, the truths that He came to this world to proclaim, and the power of your message will make itself felt." —*Testimonies for the Church*, Vol. 8, p. 300.

"His disciples are to teach only what He commanded them." —*Selected Messages*, Book One, p. 170.

"God will not excuse men for teaching theories that Christ has not taught." —Ellen G. White Manuscript 132, 1903.

"No responsible New Testament scholar would claim that the doctrine of the Trinity was taught by Jesus, or preached by the earliest Christians, or consciously held by any writer in the New Testament." —Anthony Tyrrell Hanson, *The Image of the Invisible God*. London, SCM Press, 1982, p. 87.

"It is not His plan that His people shall present something which they have to suppose, which is not taught in the Word." —*Selected Messages*, Book One, p. 174.

"The Bible does not teach the doctrine of the Trinity.... The language of the doctrine is the language of the ancient church taken from classical Greek philosophy." —Shirley Guthrie, Jr., professor of theology at Columbia Theological Seminary, *Christian Doctrine*, 1994, pp. 76–77.

"Ye shall not add unto the word which I command you, neither shall ye diminish ought from it." —Deuteronomy 4:2.

"The Old Testament does not explicitly teach that God is triune." —*Seventh-day Adventists Believe...A Biblical Exposition of 27 Fundamental Doctrines*, p. 22.

"The New Testament does not have any explicit statement on the Trinity." —Denis Fortin, "God, the Trinity and Adventism," *Perspective Digest*, Vol. 15, Issue 4.

"Scholars generally agree that there is no doctrine of the Trinity as such in either the Old Testament or the New Testament." —*The HarperCollins Encyclopedia of Catholicism*, Richard McBrien, general editor, 1995, "God," p. 564.

"There is no evidence that the apostles of Jesus ever heard of the Trinity—at any rate from him." —H. G. Wells, *The Outline of History*, The Macmillan Company, 3rd Edition, 1921, p. 499.

"Let them search the Scriptures earnestly, with a solemn realization that if they teach for doctrine the things that are not contained in God's Word, they will be as those represented in the last chapter of Revelation." —*Evangelism*, p. 214.

"It is fair to say that the Bible does not clearly teach the doctrine of the Trinity.... In fact, there is not even one proof text." —Charles Ryrie, *Basic Theology*, 1999, p. 89.

"The role of the trinity in a doctrine of God always raises questions. One reason is that the word itself does not appear in the Bible, nor is there any clear statement of the idea.... [T]he doctrine of the trinity is not part of what the Bible itself says about God...." —Richard Rice, *The Reign of God, An Introduction to Christian Theology from a Seventh-day Adventist Perspective*, Andrews University Press, 1985, p. 89.

"Neither the word 'Trinity' nor the explicit doctrine appears in the New Testament." —Trinity. *Encyclopedia Britannica*, https://www.britannica.com/topic/Trinity-Christianity (Accessed May 29, 2022).

"We must honestly admit that the doctrine of the Trinity did not form part of the early Christian—New Testament—message.... Not only the word 'Trinity', but even the explicit idea of the Trinity is absent from the apostolic witness to the faith." —Emil Brunner, *The Christian Doctrine of God*: Dogmatics, Vol. I, Philadelphia: Westminster Press, 1950, p. 205.

"So with no clear theology of the Trinity in the Bible, early Christians struggled to know how to regard Jesus and the Holy Spirit." —Loren Seibold, "The Trinity," *Signs of the Times*, December 2017, p. 45.

"No text of Scripture specifically says that God is three Persons: but theological reasoning on the basis of biblical principles leads to that conclusion." —Kwabena Donkor, Biblical Research Institute Release 9, *God in 3 Persons—in Theology*, May 2015, p. 20.

"To my ministering brethren I would say, 'Preach the word; be instant in season, out of season' (2 Tim. 4:2). Do not bring to the foundation wood, and hay, and stubble— your own surmisings and speculations, which can benefit no one. *Christ withheld no truths essential to our salvation.* Those things that are revealed are for us and our children, but we are not to allow our imagination to frame doctrines concerning things not revealed." —*Selected Messages*, Book One, p. 173.

"My conclusion, then, about the doctrine of the Trinity is that it is an artificial construct." —Cyril C. Richardson, *The Doctrine of the Trinity*, Abingdon Press, 1958, p. 148.

"But in vain they do worship me, teaching for doctrines the commandments of men." —Matthew 15:9.

"In order to be co-workers with God, in order to become like Him and to reveal His character, we must know Him aright. We must know Him as He reveals Himself."

The Ministry of Healing, p. 409

QUESTIONS FOR CONSIDERATION

In recent years many Bible students have honestly begun to question the doctrine of the Trinity. It is possible, however, to abandon one line of human reasoning, only to embrace an equally speculative conclusion on the opposite side of the issue. When controversies arise, each side wants to point out fallacies in their opponent's explanations, often without realizing that they themselves may have also ventured beyond a plain "Thus saith the Lord." But if all would simply content themselves with what God has directly told us, they could find agreement.

We are grateful for the abundant light in the Spirit of Prophecy writings, from which we learn the following:

• There are three living persons of the heavenly trio.[42]

• In Christ is life, original, unborrowed, underived.[43]

• From the days of eternity the Lord Jesus Christ was one with the Father.[44]

• The Son of God was the acknowledged Sovereign of heaven, one in power and authority with the Father.[45]

---

42   *Evangelism*, p. 615.
43   *The Desire of Ages*, p. 530.
44   *Ibid.*, p. 19.
45   *The Great Controversy*, p. 495.

- There never was a time when He was not in close fellowship with the eternal God.[46]

- [Jesus] from the beginning was equal with the Father.[47]

- Christ was God essentially, and in the highest sense. He was with God from all eternity, God over all, blessed forevermore. The Lord Jesus Christ, the divine Son of God, existed from eternity, a distinct person, yet one with the Father.[48]

- The Holy Spirit…is as much a person as God is a person.[49]

- He must also be a divine person.[50]

- The third person of the Godhead.[51]

On these points the case is settled. But do these established truths equate to the definition of "one God" as three Persons? Or does the Bible explain it differently?

I am suggesting that the Bible *does* explain it differently and that Ellen White does also. In the next few pages I'll point out those differences. Then we'll consider seven, six-word questions to help us process it all.

Trinity vs. Shared Life

The tri–unity concept of one God in three Persons is Christendom's traditional solution for fitting the revealed truths of the divinity of Jesus and the personality of the Holy Spirit into the biblical teaching of a single God. The Trinity theory is not

---

46 *Evangelism*, p. 615.
47 White, *Counsels to Parents, Teachers, and Students*, p. 13.
48 *Selected Messages*, Book One, p. 247.
49 *Evangelism*, p. 616.
50 *Ibid*., p. 617.
51 *Ibid*.

articulated in Scripture. Nevertheless, most Christian churches have adopted the formula and in fact have made it the primary test of orthodoxy.

But as we have seen, the Bible counts "one God" in a simpler, more straightforward manner:

> But to us there is but one God, *the Father*, of whom are all things, and we in him; and one Lord Jesus Christ, by whom are all things, and we by him. (1 Corinthians 8:6)

The Bible's testimony is clear and consistent. The "one God" is the Father. This, however, does not deny Jesus' divinity. "Christ is God as well as man."[52] "The Lord Jesus Christ, the only begotten Son of the Father, is *truly God in infinity, but not in personality*."[53] The *person* of God is the Father. Jesus is the Son of God, "the express image of His person."[54] The divinity of Christ is established in His *oneness* with His Father. "I and my Father are one," He said.[55] What does that mean? We understand that they are "one in nature, in character, and in purpose."[56] But it is far deeper than that. Notice carefully how Jesus explains it:

> He that hath seen me hath seen the Father; and how sayest thou then, Shew us the Father? Believest thou not that *I am in the Father, and the Father in me*? The words that I speak unto you I speak not of myself: but *the Father that dwelleth in me*, he doeth the works. Believe me that *I am in the Father, and the Father in me*: or else believe me for the very works' sake.[57]

---

52 White, 17LtMs, Lt 96, 1902, par. 28. See also John 1:1; 20:28; Hebrews 1:8.
53 White, 20LtMs, Ms 116, 1905, par. 19.
54 Hebrews 1:3
55 John 10:30
56 *The Great Controversy*, p. 493.
57 John 14:9-11

"The Father that dwelleth in me." Here Jesus provides the key to understanding divine oneness. Just as "every child lives by the life of his father,"[58] so "through the beloved Son, *the Father's life* flows out to all."[59]

So it is the Father's life that is in the Son.

> In Christ is gathered all the glory of the Father. In Him is all the fulness of the Godhead. He is the brightness of the Father's glory and the express image of His person.[60]

The crisis in Galilee (John 6) was a turning point in Christ's ministry. Following the feeding of the five thousand, the essence of Christ's message was distilled in the Bread of Life discourse. Truth, grand and broad, is encapsulated in Jesus' summary statement: "As the living Father hath sent me, and *I live by the Father:* so he that eateth me, even he shall live by me." John 6:57. Commenting on that verse, Ellen White says,

> God has sent his Son to communicate *his* own life to humanity. Christ declares, "I live by the Father," *my life and his being one.*[61]

One God means one divine life. "There is but one Way, one Truth, and one Life."[62] That life, the life of God, Jesus shares with His Father. Jesus is not a separate, independent Deity. Nor was His life generated through any process of origination. Christ's life is as eternal as the Father, for it is in fact the Father's own life.

This explains the full divinity of Jesus and His equality with the Father. We don't need to speculate as to exactly what "begotten" means, or engage in any other useless debate. If Inspi-

---

58 White, *Thoughts from the Mount of Blessing*, p. 78.
59 *The Desire of Ages*, p. 21.
60 *Signs of the Times*, November 24, 1898.
61 *The Home Missionary,* June 1, 1897.
62 *Manuscript Releases*, Vol. 2, p. 124.

ration doesn't tell us, it isn't necessary for us to know. But what we do know is that the Father and the Son share one divine life, "because it was the life of God in His Son."[63]

Thus John could write, "God hath given to us eternal life, and this life is in his Son." 1 John 5:11. And Paul could explain, "God was in Christ, reconciling the world unto himself." 2 Corinthians 5:19.[64] Divine oneness is spelled out in the Bible, not as a plurality of Persons whose "unity" lies merely in the mutual harmony and love that they enjoy, but far more meaningfully as the sharing of a single divine Life.

Let me try to clarify the difference. The Trinitarian formula says one God equals three Persons. It happens to be three, but whether there were two or four or twenty, they would still be considered one God, because the designation "one" is applied to their unity, rather than to how many Persons are included. They are one as a group. That's the standard Trinity explana-

---

63 White, *Faith and Works*, p. 22.
64 Consider the expression "God in Christ Jesus." (1 Thessalonians 5:18).
"Our heavenly Father...gave *Himself* in the person of Christ, that all who would might be saved" (White, *Steps to Christ*, p. 54).
"God gave *Himself* in His Son" (*Christ's Object Lessons*, p. 191).
"He gave *Himself* in Christ for the sin of the world" (*Christ's Object Lessons*, p. 174).
"As a remedy for the terrible consequences into which selfishness led the human race, God gave His only begotten Son to die for mankind. How could He have given more? In this gift He gave *Himself*. 'I and My Father are one,' said Christ" (*The Workers' Bulletin*, September 9, 1902).
"That this redemption might be ours, God withheld not even the sacrifice of *Himself*. He gave *Himself* in His Son. The Father suffered with Christ in all His humiliation and agony.... The human heart knows the love of a parent for his child. We know what a mother's love will do and suffer for her beloved one. But never can the heart of man fathom the depths of God's self-sacrifice. O, the cross, the cross! It is set up that we may know the only true God, and Jesus Christ whom He has sent. Only the cross can measure the length and breadth, the depth and height, of infinite love, the greatness of the Father's sacrifice for lost humanity" (*Australasian Union Conference Record*, June 1, 1900).

tion. But whenever the Bible, on the other hand, tells us who the "one God" is, it is invariably a single Being, the Father. The expression, "one God" is never defined as a unity of Persons. Thus there is only one divine life. Yet "that eternal life, which was with the Father,...was manifested unto us." 1 John 1:2. "The Word was made flesh, and dwelt among us, (and we beheld his glory, the glory as of the only begotten of the Father,) full of grace and truth." John 1:14.

But this is getting into our first question. So let's bring it on.

1. Where is the Source of Life?

All Christians recognize God as the source of life. But the concept of Trinity envisions God as made up of three members who are each self-existent. That would be three distinct sources of life. So the first question we need to ask is whether there is one ultimate source of life in the universe or three.

The Trinitarian argument contends that if only one member of the Trinity was the Source, the other two would be inferior to Him. The Shared Life view, on the other hand, suggests that divine equality does not consist merely in parity or in the possession of similar attributes, but in the actuality of a single divine life that can never be made superior or inferior to itself.

This takes us back to the original Nicene controversy. The general understanding of Christians in the early 4th century was that Jesus was the very essence of God. But Arius ascribed to Jesus a substance *like* that of the Father rather than the very substance *of* the Father. The question was not whether Jesus is a distinct Person from the Father. The point of difference was whether He is distinct in *essence*. To Arius, "the Son is *essentially* distinct from the Father."[65] This idea was rejected by the Coun-

---

65   Philip Schaff, *History of the Christian Church*, Vol. 3, § 124, "Arianism."

cil in the year 325, but it has regained influence in the theory of three independently self-existent Beings.

Let's take a look at that word "self-existent." Ellen White applied this term to Jesus a number of times.

> Silence fell upon the vast assembly. The name of God, given to Moses to express the idea of the eternal presence, had been claimed as His own by this Galilean Rabbi. He had announced Himself to be the self-existent One, He who had been promised to Israel, "whose goings forth have been from of old, from the days of eternity."[66]

Theologians have defined *self-existent* as "a term to describe any being who is divine and whose existence is understood to be not dependent on any other divine being."[67] But was Jesus' claim to self-existence an assertion that His existence was not dependent on any other divine being? Quite the contrary. As it turns out, His announcement was an affirmation of His *identity with* the Father. Ellen White tells us in the very next paragraph, it was a "claim to be one with God."[68] The very expression that is often used to support the idea that Jesus' existence is *independent* of the Father is actually an exclamation of His inseparable *oneness with* Him.

That emphasis is maintained throughout the chapter: "God is light; and in the words, 'I am the light of the world,' Christ declared His oneness with God."[69] "'I do nothing of myself....' He did not attempt to prove His Messianic claim, but showed His unity with God."[70] Jesus is teaching the exact opposite of

---

66   *The Desire of Ages*, pp. 469, 470.
67   Woodrow Whidden, Jerry Moon, John Reeve, *The Trinity: Understanding God's Love, His Plan of Salvation, and Christian Relationships* (Hagerstown: Review and Herald Publishing Association, 2002), 19.
68   *The Desire of Ages*, p. 470.
69   *Ibid.*, p. 464.
70   *Ibid.*, p. 465.

independence here. In each of His claims He is emphasizing a living connection with His Father.

The theory that Jesus' life is "not dependent on any other divine being" contradicts the inspired testimony concerning the life of the Father in the Son. Many would prefer Jesus to be His own independent source of life. But with that approach, the Father would be His own source of life, Jesus would be His own source of life, and the Holy Spirit His own source of life. That would give us three distinct sources of life in the universe. But the pen of inspiration explicitly says:

> Our Father in heaven is the source of life, of wisdom, and of joy.[71]

> The Ancient of days is God the Father.... It is He, *the source of all being*, and the fountain of all law, that is to preside in the judgment.[72]

> All things Christ received from God, but He took to give. So in the heavenly courts, in His ministry for all created beings: through the beloved Son, the Father's life flows out to all; through the Son it returns, in praise and joyous service, a tide of love, to the great Source of all.[73]

Certainly the life of Jesus is self-existent. Otherwise He would not be divine. But if the Father, Son, and Holy Spirit were each independently self-existent, they might be identical, they might be united in purpose, but they could not be organically one. They would be, in the final analysis, three separate deities working together. If you want one God, you cannot have three independent sources of life.

Ellen White explains Jesus' self-existence in terms of His

---

71   *Steps to Christ*, p. 9.
72   *The Great Controversy*, p. 479.
73   *The Desire of Ages*, p. 21.

identity with the Father. "Upon the throne with the eternal, self-existent One is He who 'hath borne our griefs, and carried our sorrows.'"[74] "The Son of God shared the Father's throne, and the glory of the eternal, self-existent One encircled both."[75] Jesus' self-existence can never be dissociated from His vital connection to His Father "of whom are all things." 1 Corinthians 8:6. The matter is settled clearly: "He declared that He had no existence separate from the Father."[76] In claiming to be the self-existent One, Jesus was claiming oneness with God.

2. Is Shared Life a Derived Life?

In Christ is life, original, unborrowed, underived. (*The Desire of Ages*, p. 530)

Some have assumed an incompatibility between that inspired statement and Jesus' own words in John 5:26, "For as the Father hath life in himself; so hath he given to the Son to have life in himself." They figure that if the Father "gave" to the Son to have life, then Jesus' life would be "derived." For this reason, John 5:26 is often explained as referring only to Jesus' earthly life, not to His pre-existent life. By the same rule, any mention of inheritance (Hebrews 1:4), or any reference to the life of the Father in the Son (1 John 5:11), is also applied to His humanity, not to His eternal divinity. The rationale is that those verses, if applied to His pre-incarnational life, would violate the rule of "underived." Therefore all the inspired descriptions of the shared life relationship between the Father and the Son are dismissed as pertaining only to the incarnated Christ.

The proponents of that line of reasoning may not realize the implications of that position. By insisting that Jesus shared

---

74 *The Great Controversy*, p. 416.

75 White, *Patriarchs and Prophets*, p. 36.

76 White, "Christ Revealed the Father," *Review and Herald*, January 7, 1890, par. 1.

His Father's life only upon His incarnation, and by supposing a shared life to be a derived life, they are unwittingly assigning to Jesus a derived life while on earth.

But the context of the statement declaring Christ's life to be underived (*The Desire of Ages*, p. 530) was the raising of Lazarus. Jesus was not talking about a former life, but of His power to impart life at that very moment, when He proclaimed, "I am the resurrection, and the life." It was in amplification of that announcement that the servant of the Lord wrote, "In Christ is life, original, unborrowed, underived." Jesus did not relinquish His underivedness by taking on humanity. Standing before the sepulcher of Lazarus, Jesus had life, original, unborrowed, underived.

Jesus can thus partake of the life of His Father,[77] as the inspired record tells us, while *at the same time* the life is described as "unborrowed and underived." The Father's life "given to the Son" (John 5:26) is not a derived life. Hence, the often-quoted statement in *The Desire of Ages* page 530 does not rule out a shared life between the Father and the Son.

The Saviour's life was never "derived." Strong acids are derived from the combustion of fossil fuels. Heroin is derived by modifying the molecular structure of morphine. But Jesus' life is not a derivative. It is the original, underived life of God; the genuine article.

3. Does "Son of God" Indicate Humanity?

The term "son of God" is applied in the Bible variously to people, to angels, and to Christ. But its application to Christ is unique.

---

77 "As a man He supplicated the throne of God till His humanity was charged with a heavenly current that should connect humanity with divinity. Through continual communion *He received life from God*, that He might impart life to the world" (*The Desire of Ages*, p. 363).

"He gave his only-begotten Son,"—not a son by creation, as were the angels, nor a son by adoption, as is the forgiven sinner, but a Son begotten in the express image of the Father's person, and in all the brightness of his majesty and glory, one equal with God in authority, dignity, and divine perfection. In him dwelt all the fullness of the Godhead bodily.[78]

Here is the question: Is the expression "Son of God" applicable to Christ only in light of His incarnation? If He had never become the Son of Man, would He still have been the Son of God? Or is this title a product or reflection of His humanity?

The general opinion of scholars is that the Bible's references to Jesus as God's Son are all in light of His incarnation.[79] In other words, Jesus would not have been the Son of God had He not come to earth as a human. But is this explanation consistent with the context of the title's usage? For example, the *Signs of the Times* reference quoted above says that Jesus was a Son begotten in all the brightness of the Father's majesty and glory. If "Son of God" has to do with Jesus' coming into this world, did He come to earth in all the brightness of the Father's majesty and glory? Not at all. For if He had, sinners could not have endured His presence.

God's declaration of Jesus as "my beloved Son"[80] was not a statement of Jesus' humanity, but rather it was "the voice of

---

78 *Signs of the Times*, May 30, 1895.
79 "The Father-Son relationship in the New Testament must always be understood in the light of the event of Bethlehem. The only child born into this world with a divine, rather than a human, father is Jesus. The title, 'Son' refers to His entry into time and does not deny at all His eternal origin. There are references in the Old Testament to Sonship, but these are always in anticipation of the Incarnation." —J. R. Hoffman, *Ministry*, June 1982, p. 24. "Thus, the idea of Jesus as God's 'only begotten Son' is not dealing with the nature of Christ as deity but with His role in the plan of salvation." —*The Message of Hebrews,* Adult Sabbath School Bible Study Guide for January 13, 2022.
80 Matthew 3:17

Jehovah testifying to the *divinity* of Jesus."[81] I'd like to give evidence that the title "Son of God" has nothing at all to do with Jesus' humanity, but that it pointedly expresses His divinity, His equality with the Father, His true oneness with God.

When Jesus was brought before the Sanhedrin for healing the man by the pool of Bethesda on the Sabbath, He answered, "My Father worketh hitherto, and I work." John 5:17. But this answer only gave the rulers a greater case against Him. "Therefore the Jews sought the more to kill him, because he not only had broken the Sabbath, but said also that God was his Father, making himself equal with God." Verse 18. The Jews recognized that to be the Son of God is to be equal with God. "Jesus...in calling God 'His own Father' had declared Himself equal with God."[82]

If, as it is claimed, the "Father/Son" language of the Bible in reference to God and Jesus is merely in light of the Incarnation—if God was Jesus' Father only in His humanity—then Jesus' statement would not have been considered blasphemous.

> The whole nation of the Jews called God their Father, therefore they would not have been so enraged if Christ had represented Himself as standing in the same relation to God. But they accused Him of blasphemy, showing that they understood Him as making this claim in the highest sense.[83]

Jesus' divine authority resides in His position as the Son of God. "My authority, He said, for doing the work of which you accuse Me, is that I am the Son of God."[84] Because Lucifer was "unwilling to submit to the *authority* of Jesus,"[85] he wanted to

---

81 *The Desire of Ages*, p. 116.
82 *Ibid.*, p. 207.
83 *Ibid.*, pp. 207, 208.
84 *Ibid.*, p. 208.
85 White, *Spiritual Gifts*, vol. 1, pp. 17, 18.

"obscure [the fact] that Christ was the only begotten Son of God."[86] This defiance was evident in the taunt, "If thou be the Son of God."[87] By challenging Christ's Sonship he was denying His authority.

On Jesus' final day of teaching in the temple, one question after another was put to Him in an attempt to come up with some pretext for condemning Him to death. Finally, Jesus posed a question to His interrogators that silenced them.

"What think ye of Christ? Whose son is He?"[88] Jesus' questions were never unimportant. But when we examine the dynamics of this exchange, this was in all likelihood the most weighty question He ever asked. "Whose Son is He?"

Their ready answer, "The Son of David," expressed merely His humanity.

> But many who called Jesus the Son of David did not recognize His divinity. They did not understand that the Son of David was also the Son of God.[89]

> This question was designed to test their belief concerning the Messiah,—to show whether they regarded Him simply as a man or as the Son of God.[90]

Just a few days later, Jesus was standing on trial before the high priest. One false witness after another was brought in, "but neither so did their witness agree together." Mark 14:59. Throughout the trial Jesus remained silent.

Caiaphas was becoming desperate. At last he demanded, "I adjure thee by the living God, that thou tell us whether thou be the Christ, *the Son of God*." Matthew 26:63.

---

86   White, *This Day With God*, p. 128.
87   Matthew 4:3, 6; 27:40.
88   Matthew 22:42
89   *The Desire of Ages*, p. 609.
90   *Ibid.*, p. 608.

The fate of the Accused hinged on His response here. But "more than this, *His own relation to the Father* was called in question. He must *plainly* declare His character and mission."[91] This was no time for an ambiguous answer. No place for metaphors or potential misunderstandings. He will "plainly" acknowledge "His own relation to the Father."

"And Jesus said, I am." Mark 14:62.

"Then the high priest rent his clothes, saying, He hath spoken blasphemy; what further need have we of witnesses? Behold, now ye have heard his blasphemy." Matthew 26:65.

This scene was repeated when the Sanhedrin later assembled legally in the light of day. Again the pivotal question was asked, "Art thou then the Son of God? And he said unto them, Ye say that I am." Luke 22:70.

This confession was the legal basis for His crucifixion. "He had declared Himself the Son of God."[92] The Jews finally had one legitimate accusation to present to Pilate. "We have a law, and by our law he ought to die, because he made himself the Son of God." John 19:7.

Just a few months earlier the Jews had tried to take Christ's life because of His claim, "I and My Father are one." John 10:30. They saw that as blasphemy, "because that thou, being a man, makest thyself God." Verse 33.

Jesus replied, "Say ye of him, whom the Father hath sanctified, and sent into the world, Thou blasphemest; because I said, I am the Son of God?" Verse 36. "The Father is in me, and I in him." Verse 38.

Thus Jesus made clear the connection between the oneness of the Father and the Son, the divinity of Christ, His position as the Son of God, and the shared life between them.

Popular theological interpretation reduces the term "Son

---

91   *Ibid.*, p. 706.
92   *Ibid.*, p. 714.

of God" to a mere figure of speech, a metaphor. But the Bible presents Christ's Sonship as the very explanation of His divinity. It is *as* the Son of God that Jesus is one with the Father. It is *as* the Son of God that He shares His Father's life. It is no wonder that this expression becomes the essential Christian confession of faith throughout the New Testament.[93]

Ellen White dismissed any notion of figurative language on this point:

> The scriptures *clearly* indicate the relation between God and Christ, and they bring to view as clearly the personality and individuality of each. "God, who at sundry times and in divers manners spake in time past unto the fathers by the prophets, hath in these last days spoken unto us by *His Son*, whom He hath appointed heir of all things, by whom also He made the worlds; who being the brightness of glory, and the express image of His person, and upholding all things by the word of His power, when He had by Himself purged our sins, sat down on the right hand of the Majesty on high; being made so much better than the angels, as He hath by inheritance obtained a more excellent name than they. For unto which of the angels said He at any time, Thou art My Son, this day have I begotten Thee? And again, I will be to Him a Father, and He shall be to Me a Son?" Hebrews 1:1-5.
>
> God is the Father of Christ; Christ is the Son of God. To Christ has been given an exalted position. He has been made equal with the Father. All the counsels of God are opened to His Son.[94]

To treat the title "Son of God" as an expression of Jesus' humanity or as meaning anything less than full inherent ownership of the eternal life of God, is to deprive of its meaning the

---

93   This will be demonstrated in the next chapter.
94   *Testimonies for the Church*, Vol. 8, p. 268.

clearest and most expressive statement of His divinity.

4. Was Jesus a Mediator From Eternity?

> For there is one God, and one mediator between God
> and men, the man Christ Jesus. (1 Timothy 2:5)

My fourth question addresses the intrinsic identity of Christ. A common belief is that the Father, Son, and Holy Spirit had no original, inherent distinction in role or function.[95] It is believed that at some point in the past a determination was made as to what role each of them would subsequently assume in relation to creation and redemption.[96] Since that time they have each performed slightly different tasks, but those differences are somewhat arbitrarily assigned. The Father is not in real life the Father, and the Son is not really the Son—other than in the artificial roles they have each chosen to play.

Jesus, according to this reasoning, did not originally have a distinctive mediatorial identity. That role was chosen by or assigned to Him through some process at some point in time. These are the assumptions of the doctrine of the Trinity.

But what does Inspiration say?

> *From everlasting* He was the Mediator of the covenant, the
> one in whom all nations of the earth, both Jews and Gen-
> tiles, if they accepted Him, were to be blessed.[97]

So we see that Jesus' mediatorial identity was not a product of His incarnation. Long before mediation was necessary, there

---

95 J. R. Spangler described this as "the interchangeableness of the members of the Godhead" (J. R. Spangler, "I Believe in the Triune God," *Review and Herald*, October 21, 1971, p. 8).

96 See Gordon Jenson, "Jesus, the Heavenly Intercessor," *Adventist Review*, October 31, 1996, p. 12; and Frank B. Holbrook, "Frank Answers," *Signs of the Times*, July, 1985.

97 *Selected Messages*, Book One, p. 247.

was a Mediator. He was such, in fact, "from everlasting." Those who wish to make His mediatorial singularity an add-on, rather than the distinctive character of who He naturally is, would need to find some way to redefine "everlasting" if they wish to maintain their view that Jesus was not eternally, inherently the Mediator.

The two expressions "from everlasting" and "from eternity" are synonymous. And in this very context Ellen White says, "The Lord Jesus Christ, the divine Son of God, existed *from eternity*, a distinct person, yet one with the Father."[98] To argue against Him being the Mediator "from everlasting" is to question His existence "from eternity," for both are asserted by Inspiration.

But once we acknowledge an innate mediatorial character in Christ to eternally differentiate His position from that of the Father, the whole theory of arbitrary role assignments deflates. The positions of the Father and the Son have never been transposable.

The time prophecy of Daniel 12:11 pinpoints the year in which Christ's perpetual mediatorial role would be theologically "taken away." In AD 508 the doctrine of the Trinity triumphed militarily in Europe.[99] The imposed doctrine takes away from Jesus His eternal mediatorial identity.

5. Can Extrabiblical Propositions Be Made Tests?

The Seventh-day Adventist Church Manual identifies thirteen "reasons for which members shall be subject to discipline." The first of these is "Denial of faith in the fundamentals of the gospel and in the fundamental beliefs of the Church or teaching

---

98   *Ibid.*
99   William H. Shea, *Daniel: A Reader's Guide* (Nampa: Pacific Press Publishing Association, 2005), 274.

doctrines contrary to the same."[100]

Certainly, one who is a devout Seventh-day Adventist has chosen this church because he loves the Lord and is committed to the distinctive message for which this denomination was called into existence. He embraces the fundamental beliefs (not capitalized) of the church. To deny those beliefs would be inconsistent with his membership. But when we speak of the Fundamental Beliefs (capitalized) of Seventh-day Adventists, we are referring to an official document by that name that has been voted by the world church in General Conference Session. The document contains specific wording that has been approved for official publication.

Some have interpreted the *Manual's* first reason for discipline to mean that a member must, as a test of fellowship, affirm the precise wording of the official Fundamental Beliefs statement. If that were the case, the document itself, rather than the Bible, would become the standard, the criterion, by which one's beliefs must be judged.

When it comes to Fundamental Belief #2, nearly everyone acknowledges that that formulation is not presented in the Bible as such.[101] It is merely a human attempt to synthesize what is believed to be the teaching of Scripture. This brings us to our question as to the appropriateness of requiring doctrinal conclusions that are not stated in the inspired writings. The question is, Is it proper to impose our synthesis on our members, and discipline those who do not agree with our reasoning,

---

100 "Reasons for Discipline," *Seventh-day Adventist Church Manual* (2015), p. 62.

101 "There are topics such as the Trinity…that deal with biblical-theological concepts which cannot directly or at least not exclusively be based on biblical vocabulary…. There is no biblical text that says: 'There is one God in three persons, Father, Son, and Holy Spirit.'" —Ekkehardt Mueller, "Hermeneutical Guidelines for Dealing with Theological Questions," *Reflections*, #40, October 2012 (Biblical Research Institute, General Conference of Seventh-day Adventists), p. 1.

even though those members may accept everything the Bible actually says? Which should be the test, the Bible itself or the theologians' ideas of what the Bible means?

The answers to these questions depend upon how much authority the church has been granted in regard to the establishment of doctrine. Ellen White makes it clear that the General Conference in Session is God's highest authority on earth.

> At times, when a small group of men entrusted with the general *management* of the work have, in the name of the General Conference, sought to carry out unwise *plans* and to restrict God's work, I have said that I could no longer regard the voice of the General Conference, represented by these few men, as the voice of God. But this is not saying that the decisions of a General Conference composed of an assembly of duly appointed, representative men from all parts of the field, should not be respected. God has ordained that the representatives of His church from all parts of the earth, when assembled in a General Conference, shall have authority.[102]

> I have been shown that no man's judgment should be surrendered to the judgment of any one man. But when the judgment of the General Conference, which is the highest authority that God has upon the earth, is exercised, private independence and private judgment must not be maintained, but be surrendered.[103]

But does that authority extend to the formulation of doctrine? Whenever Ellen White emphasizes the authority that God has placed in the General Conference Session, the immediate context is always operational and policy decisions—the *management* of the work. Notice as we continue reading:

---

102 White, *Gospel Workers*, p. 490.
103 *Testimonies for the Church*, Vol. 3, p. 492.

> Your error was in persistently maintaining your private
> judgment of your *duty* against the voice of the highest au-
> thority the Lord has upon the earth.[104]

"Your duty." Duty would be obligatory tasks, actions, or re-
sponsibilities. It doesn't sound like she's talking about doctrine
here. The same is true with the quotation we cited just above
that, which continues with the following sentence:

> The error that some are in danger of committing, is in
> giving to the mind and judgment of one man, or of a small
> group of men, the full measure of authority and influence
> that God has vested in His church, in the judgment and
> voice of the General Conference assembled *to plan for the
> prosperity and advancement of His work.*[105]

The General Conference is responsible for making decisions
as to how the work is to be carried forward. Its quinquennial
Session is the voice of God in regard to the execution of our
assigned task. It establishes the policies that direct our united
efforts. But I haven't found a single inspired statement that says
the church is authorized to formulate doctrine. That job be-
longs only to God. "He Himself has taught us what is truth."[106]
He has plainly told us everything we need to know about Him.
Our task is simply to read and believe what He has said.

But Ellen White does directly address the question of how
much authority the church has in the establishment of doctrine:

> The Roman Church reserves to the clergy the right to
> interpret the Scriptures. On the ground that ecclesiastics
> alone are competent to explain God's word, it is with-
> held from the common people. Though the Reformation
> gave the Scriptures to all, yet the selfsame principle which

---

104 *Ibid.*
105 *Gospel Workers*, p. 490.
106 *Selected Messages*, Book One, p. 161.

was maintained by Rome prevents multitudes in Protestant churches from searching the Bible for themselves. They are taught to accept its teachings *as interpreted by the church*; and there are thousands who dare receive nothing, however plainly revealed in Scripture, that is contrary to their creed or the established teaching of their church.[107]

But God will have a people upon the earth to maintain the Bible, and the Bible only, as the standard of all doctrines and the basis of all reforms. The opinions of learned men, the deductions of science, the creeds or decisions of ecclesiastical councils, as numerous and discordant as are the churches which they represent, the voice of the majority—not one nor all of these should be regarded as evidence for or against any point of religious faith. Before accepting any doctrine or precept, we should demand a plain "Thus saith the Lord" in its support.[108]

Very many will get up some test that is not given in the word of God. We have our test in the Bible,—the commandments of God and the testimony of Jesus Christ.[109]

In the commission to His disciples, Christ not only outlined their work, but *gave them their message*. Teach the people, He said, "to observe all things whatsoever I have commanded you." The disciples were to teach what Christ had taught. That which He had spoken, not only in person, but through all the prophets and teachers of the Old Testament, is here included. Human teaching is shut out. There is no place for tradition, for man's theories and conclusions, or for church legislation. No laws ordained by ecclesiastical authority are included in the commission. None of these are Christ's servants to teach.[110]

---

107 *The Great Controversy*, p. 596, emphasis hers.
108 *Ibid.*, p. 595.
109 *General Conference Bulletin*, April 16, 1901 par. 8.
110 *The Desire of Ages*, p. 826.

That answers our question. Church rulings carry no weight at all in determining what is truth. God, through His prophets, has already told us in plain language just what we are to believe and how we are to understand it. And whatever He hasn't told us, is not to concern us. The nature of the Holy Spirit, for example, is not a testing truth.[111]

> The revelation of Himself that God has given in His word is for our study. But beyond this we are not to penetrate. The highest intellect may tax itself until it is wearied out in conjectures regarding the nature of God, but the effort will be fruitless. *This problem has not been given us to solve.*[112]

> Do not try to explain in regard to the personality of God. You cannot give any further explanation than the Bible has given. Human theories regarding Him are good for nothing.[113]

"Preach the word." 2 Timothy 4:2.

6. Is the Bible a Sufficient Rule?

Supposing they were helping to protect the sacredness of the Sabbath, the Pharisees instituted regulations that God had never given. Similarly, the ecclesiastical authorities of the dark ages imposed duties that God did not require. In each instance, the leaders were implying in their legislation that the Scriptures did not sufficiently address the need. They presumed to supplement the word of God with their own teachings. But what was the result?

---

111 "The nature of the Holy Spirit is a mystery. Men cannot explain it, because the Lord has not revealed it to them." "It is not essential for us to be able to define just what the Holy Spirit is." —White, *The Acts of the Apostles*, pp. 52, 51.

112 White, *The Ministry of Healing*, p. 429.

113 White, *Counsels to Writers and Editors*, p. 94.

Rome began by enjoining what God had not forbidden, and she ended by forbidding what He had explicitly enjoined.[114]

This practice of augmenting what God has said, dates back to the course of Eve. Thinking she was defending God's word, she told the serpent, "But of the fruit of the tree which is in the midst of the garden, God hath said, Ye shall not eat of it, neither shall ye touch it, lest ye die." Genesis 3:3. Here Eve overstated the words of God's command.[115] By adding to God's words, Eve gave Satan the advantage. When he then placed the fruit in her hand and she did not die from touching it, she was emboldened to eat it.

> Add thou not unto his words, lest he reprove thee, and thou be found a liar. (Proverbs 30:6)

Years ago I learned an important lesson from an old book on how to give Bible studies:

> We sometimes have an idea, and to prove that idea we have to put it largely into our own words; that is, we do not have a plain "Thus saith the Lord" for it. *Let us omit such points.*[116]

That counsel has had a lifelong impact upon my ministry. Seriously, if the Bible doesn't say it, what makes us think we need to?

> In all the sermons and in all the Bible studies, let the people see that on every point a plain "Thus saith the Lord" is given for the faith and doctrines which we advocate.[117]

---

114 *The Great Controversy*, p. 290.

115 See White. *Confrontation*, p. 14.

116 General Conference of Seventh-day Adventists, c. 1930, *How to Give Bible Readings*, p. 41.

117 *Evangelism*, p. 153.

A doctrine that has not a "Thus saith the Lord" may be accepted by the whole world, but that does not make it truth.[118]

The great Protestant principle is that the Bible is a sufficient rule of faith and practice. But if we must add our ideas to it in order to fully present the truth, then the Bible is not sufficient. Has God not done a good enough job?

God has spoken *in the plainest language* upon every subject that affects the salvation of the soul.[119]

Matters of vital importance have been *plainly revealed* in the Word of God.[120]

No truth essential to our salvation is withheld.[121]

Those who suppose that they understand philosophy think that their explanations are necessary to unlock the treasures of knowledge and to prevent heresies from coming into the church. But it is these explanations that have brought in false theories and heresies. Men have made desperate efforts to explain what they thought to be intricate scriptures; but too often their efforts have only darkened that which they tried to make clear.[122]

The Bible with its precious gems of truth was not written for the scholar alone. On the contrary, it was designed for the common people; and the interpretation given by the common people, when aided by the Holy Spirit, accords best with the truth as it is in Jesus.[123]

---

118 White, *That I May Know Him*, p. 357.
119 White, *Review and Herald*, February 5, 1901.
120 *Selected Messages*, Book One, p. 173.
121 *The Desire of Ages*, p. 57.
122 *Christ's Object Lessons*, p. 110.
123 *Testimonies for the Church*, Vol. 5, p. 331.

If the Bible is truly sufficient, then our theological formulations are unnecessary. But to insist on the necessity of a conclusion that is never drawn by an inspired writer is essentially to deny the completeness and sufficiency of divine revelation.

7. How Authoritative Are Ellen White's Writings?

This question is central to the discussion of Adventist biblical hermeneutics. Let's consider three possible approaches a person could take to this question of Ellen White's authority in regard to the doctrine of God:

1. Ellen White was a wonderful devotional writer, but you cannot take her doctrinal statements as authoritative.

2. Ellen White's doctrinal statements must be used selectively.

3. All of Ellen White's published writings must be understood as inspired truth.

What about the first option? While this might appear to project a high view of Scripture, it actually requires a denial of the Bible passages that describe the role of the gift of prophecy in the church. Prophecy is one of the gifts of the Spirit mentioned in Ephesians 4:11. These gifts were given to prevent us from being "tossed to and fro, and carried about with every wind of doctrine." Verse 14. If we take the position that Ellen White's writings are not doctrinally trustworthy, the prophetic gift cannot do for us what the text promises.

Ellen White claimed that the light God gave her was determinative in regard to doctrine:

> The visions that the Lord has given me are so remarkable that we know that what we have accepted is the truth. This was demonstrated by the Holy Spirit. Light, precious light from God, established the main points of our faith as

we hold them today.[124]

> At that time one error after another pressed in upon us; ministers and doctors brought in new doctrines. We would search the Scriptures with much prayer, and the Holy Spirit would bring the truth to our minds.... *The power of God would come upon me, and I was enabled clearly to define what is truth and what is error. As the points of our faith were thus established*, our feet were placed upon a solid foundation. We accepted the truth point by point, *under the demonstration of the Holy Spirit. I would be taken off in vision, and explanations would be given me.* I was given illustrations of heavenly things, and of the sanctuary, so that we were placed where light was shining on us in clear, distinct rays.[125]

Because of claims like that, we either have to accept the doctrinal authority of Ellen White's writings, or we have to reject her inspiration altogether. If she was not given doctrinal instruction for the church, then she was a liar for claiming such and must be rejected entirely.

The second of the three options listed above has been adopted by certain ones on both sides of the Trinitarian debate. Some anti-Trinitarians have questioned the authenticity of certain Ellen White statements that they feel have been tampered with. Others, on the opposite side, deny the authority of Ellen White's early non-Trinitarian statements. It seems that, with both classes, if the statement doesn't agree with their own personal conclusions, it must not be from God. Thus they end up with a selective acceptance of Ellen White's writings.

One standard explanation is that Ellen White's understanding of God matured over the years and that her writings reflect that development. Thus it is implied that her later writings

---

124 *Manuscript Releases*, Vol. 8, p. 319 (1906).
125 *Ibid.* pp. 319, 320; *Gospel Workers*, p. 302.

ought to receive our primary attention in attempting to piece together the true picture of God. While I am sure her understanding of this subject grew just as did her knowledge in every other line of truth, this explanation carries the subtle suggestion that her earlier writings are less than dependable. A lack of detail in her early writings would be one thing. But an insinuation of inaccuracy therein is something entirely different and becomes a serious charge. It throws doubt on her inspiration as a whole and opens the door to a rejection of other things she wrote.

One Adventist author anticipates meeting Ellen White in heaven and asking her about her early years as an Adventist. This is what he expects to hear her say:

> I was very young then and somewhat immature. I reported things as I understood them to be. I was no doubt influenced by my husband and other associates and I also had visions from God. I can see now that I had some dreams as well as visions and mistakenly interpreted them to be visions too. As I grew in knowledge and understanding I came to see who Jesus was really and I also came to understand that the Holy Spirit was a Divine Person too. Gradually, I became a Trinitarian and I think I made this very clear in my later writings.[126]

Ellen White in heaven is thus imagined to discredit her own writings and attribute some of them to mistaken opinions. Yet, in her lifetime she clearly repudiated the suggestion that some of her writings reflected her own personal ideas:

> Some who wish to strengthen their own position will bring forward from the *Testimonies* statements which they think will support their views, and will put the strongest

---

126 Max Hatton, www.thetrinitydoctrine.com/articles/ellen-g-white-and-the-trinity-doctrine (Accessed May 29, 2022).

possible construction upon them; but that which questions their course of action, or which does not coincide with their views, they pronounce Sister White's opinion, denying its heavenly origin and placing it on a level with their own judgment.[127]

In these letters which I write, in the testimonies I bear, I am presenting to you that which the Lord has presented to me. *I do not write one article in the paper expressing merely my own ideas.* They are what God has opened before me in vision—the precious rays of light shining from the throne.[128]

I am now looking over my diaries and copies of letters written for several years back.... I have the most precious matter to reproduce and place before the people in testimony form. While I am able to do this work, the people must have things to revive past history, that they may see that there is one straight chain of truth, *without one heretical sentence*, in that which I have written. This, I am instructed, is to be a living letter to all in regard to my faith.[129]

Ellen White clearly condemned the selective acceptance of her writings.

Do not feel that you can dissect them to suit your own ideas, claiming that God has given you ability to discern what is light from heaven and what is the expression of mere human wisdom. If the *Testimonies* speak not according to the word of God, reject them. Christ and Belial cannot be united.[130]

We must conclude, then, that all of Ellen White's published

---

127 *Testimonies for the Church*, Vol. 5, p. 688.
128 *Ibid.*, p. 67.
129 *Selected Messages*, Book Three, p. 52.
130 *Testimonies for the Church*, Vol. 5, p. 691.

writings are to be received as inspired truth. Throughout her lifetime she received more and more light, but none of that light must be construed to contradict any of the statements she made under inspiration in her earlier years. If our ideas cannot be reconciled with any of her writings, it is our views that must be adjusted.

Where Do We Go From Here?

Before the day of Pentecost the disciples "put away all differences."[131] The word "all" would have to include doctrinal differences. But how in such a diverse church can that be done today?

A few lines down on the same page it says, "Let Christians put away their dissensions." And here it tells us exactly how to do it. In the preceding sentence we are told: "Instead of man's speculations, let the word of God be preached."

Inspiration clearly identifies the cause of doctrinal dissension:

> In the professedly Christian world many turn away from the plain teachings of the Bible and build up a creed from human speculations.... If the professed followers of Christ would accept God's standard, it would bring them into unity; but so long as human wisdom is exalted above His Holy Word, there will be divisions and dissension.[132]

Differences of belief thrive when explanations are urged that are not found in the inspired writings. But if we will hold to what God, through His prophets, has clearly stated, we will find agreement.

The lesson from the disciples' preparation for Pentecost is crucial. The unity that precedes the latter rain will not be based

---

131 *The Desire of Ages*, p. 827.
132 *Patriarchs and Prophets*, p. 124.

on philosophical theories or framed theological expressions. "For he whom God hath sent speaketh *the words of God.*" John 3:34.

In Ephesians 4:13 the apostle outlines the goal of the gospel:

> Till we all come in the unity of the faith, and of the knowledge of the Son of God, unto a perfect man, unto the measure of the stature of the fulness of Christ.

The measure of the stature of the fullness of Christ is the ultimate objective. That is the perfect man. But we can only reach that goal when we come in the unity of the faith. That means doctrinal unity. And we can only come in the unity of the faith when we come in the knowledge of the Son of God. When the knowledge of the Son of God is restored, we will be able to come in the unity of the faith unto a perfect man, and the work of the gospel can be finished.

THE ESSENTIAL CHRISTIAN CONFESSION OF FAITH

"What think ye of Christ? *Whose Son is He?*"
Matthew 22:42

"Whosoever shall confess that Jesus is *the Son of God*,
God dwelleth in him, and he in God." 1 John 4:15

Q. **To what did John the Baptist bear record? John 1:34**
A. "And I saw, and bare record that *this is the Son of God.*"

Q. **What did Nathanael confess? John 1:49**
A. "Nathanael answered and saith unto him, Rabbi, *thou art the Son of God*; thou art the King of Israel."

Q. **What was Peter's great confession? Matthew 16:16**
A. "And Simon Peter answered and said, Thou art the Christ, *the Son of the living God.*"

Q. **What did all the disciples assert? Matthew 14:33; John 6:69**
A. "Then they that were in the ship came and worshipped him, saying, Of a truth *thou art the Son of God.*"
A. "And we believe and are sure that thou art that Christ, *the Son of the living God.*"

Q. **What was Martha's testimony? John 11:27**

A. "She saith unto him, Yea, Lord: I believe that thou art the Christ, *the Son of God*, which should come into the world."

Q. **What did God Himself declare at Jesus' baptism? Mark 1:11**

A. "And there came a voice from heaven, saying, *Thou art my beloved Son*, in whom I am well pleased."

Q. **What truth did Satan challenge? Luke 4:3, 9**

A. "And the devil said unto him, *If thou be the Son of God*, command this stone that it be made bread."

A. "And he brought him to Jerusalem, and set him on a pinnacle of the temple, and said unto him, *If thou be the Son of God*, cast thyself down from hence."

Q. **At Christ's transfiguration, what did God again plainly declare? Matthew 17:5**

A. "While he yet spake, behold, a bright cloud overshadowed them: and behold a voice out of the cloud, which said, *This is my beloved Son*, in whom I am well pleased; hear ye him."

Q. **Why did the Jews condemn Jesus? John 10:36; 19:7**

A. "Say ye of him, whom the Father hath sanctified, and sent into the world, Thou blasphemest; because I said, *I am the Son of God?*"

A. "The Jews answered him, We have a law, and by our law he ought to die, because he made himself *the Son of God.*"

Q. **What was the issue at His trial? Luke 22:70**

A. "Then said they all, Art thou then *the Son of God?*"

Q. **What doubt was hurled at Christ on the cross? Matthew 27:40**

A. "*If thou be the Son of God*, come down from the cross."

Q. **What did the Centurion confess? Matthew 27:54**

A. "Now when the centurion, and they that were with him, watching Jesus, saw the earthquake, and those things that were done, they feared greatly, saying, *Truly this was the Son of God.*"

Q. **What does Christ's resurrection declare about Him? Romans 1:4**

A. "And declared to be *the Son of God* with power, according to the spirit of holiness, by the resurrection from the dead."

Q. **What truth did the Ethiopian eunuch believe? Acts 8:37**

A. "And Philip said, If thou believest with all thine heart, thou mayest. And he answered and said, *I believe that Jesus Christ is the Son of God.*"

Q. **What was Paul's message? Acts 9:20**

A. "And straightway he preached Christ in the synagogues, that *he is the Son of God.*"

Q. **What was the burden of John's gospel? John 20:31**

A. "But these are written, that ye might believe that Jesus is the Christ, *the Son of God*; and that believing ye might have life through his name."

Q. **Who can overcome the world? 1 John 5:5**

A. "Who is he that overcometh the world, but he that believeth that *Jesus is the Son of God?*"

Q. **What question is left for us? John 9:35**

A. "Dost thou believe on *the Son of God?*"

"The flashing forth of His divinity in the cleansing of the temple, His miracles of healing, and the lessons of divine truth that fell from His lips, all proclaimed that which after the healing at Bethesda He had declared before the Sanhedrin,—His Sonship to the Eternal."

The Desire of Ages, p. 231

WHY IT MATTERS

"But I fear, lest by any means, as the serpent beguiled
Eve through his subtilty, so your minds should be
corrupted from the *simplicity* that is in Christ."
2 Corinthians 11:3

Throughout this book we've emphasized the fact that *God Himself has taken on the personal responsibility of teaching His people what is truth*. And that includes the truth about Himself. We also know just how He accomplishes it:

> If there be a prophet among you, *I the Lord will make my-self known unto him* in a vision, and will speak unto him in a dream. (Numbers 12:6)

> Surely the Lord God will do nothing, but he revealeth his secret unto his servants the prophets. (Amos 3:7)

God has not left any essential truth for us to figure out ourselves. He is the best Teacher there ever was. To the prophets He has explained everything we need to know, making it *plain* and *clear*. And when those holy men of God spake as they were moved by the Holy Ghost, there was no uncertainty.

But the greatest revelation of God to man was in the person of His Son. Jesus came to reveal God, and He did not fail in that mission. There is not a more dependable source of truth about God than the words of Jesus Himself. "Christ's sayings are pure gold without one particle of dross."[133]

---

133 *Counsels to Parents, Teachers, and Students*, p. 430.

Few realize the full force of Christ's words in regard to His connection with the Father.[134]

His utterances were *clear* and *plain*.[135]

But Satan has ever worked and is still working with all deceivableness of unrighteousness to make the Word of God of none effect. He seeks to make mysterious that which is *simple* and *plain*.[136]

It was his policy to perplex with subtle arguments concerning the purposes of God. Everything that was *simple* he shrouded in *mystery*, and by artful perversion cast doubt upon the *plainest* statements of Jehovah.[137]

Satan has worked to undermine our confidence in the sure word of prophecy and in the words of Christ Himself. One "dangerous error is the doctrine that denies the deity of Christ, claiming that He had no existence before His advent to this world."[138] The problem is that "it directly contradicts *the plainest statements of our Saviour concerning His relationship with the Father*."[139]

Let's not miss that point. The way we can know if a doctrine concerning Christ is "dangerous error," is if it "directly contradicts the *plainest* statements of our Saviour concerning His relationship with the Father." This means that the way Jesus explained His relationship to the Father must be accepted as the infallible standard by which we may distinguish truth from error on this subject.

---

134 White, *The Spirit of Prophecy*, Vol. 2, p. 166.

135 *Ibid.*, p. 167.

136 *Selected Messages*, Book One, p. 345.

137 *Patriarchs and Prophets*, p. 41.

138 *The Great Controversy*, p. 524.

139 *Ibid.*

If men reject *the testimony of the inspired Scriptures* concerning the deity of Christ, it is in vain to argue the point with them; for no argument, however conclusive, could convince them.[140]

We have cause for concern when we see human explanations being given more authority than the plain words of Jesus. In this chapter we will summarize some of those concerns and point out why those things matter.

The Current Issue

Although "Seventh-day Adventists accept the Bible as their only creed,"[141] some local churches have used the statement of Fundamental Beliefs as if it were a creed. When a statement of beliefs designed for informational purposes is improperly used as the standard for discipline, it becomes a creed. Such misuse often leads to sharp division in the church.

Before we go any further, we need to clarify our definition of "Trinity" and "Trinitarian." A correct belief in the divinity, personality, oneness, eternity, and equality of the Father, Son, and Holy Spirit—most Adventists fall into this category—does not of itself make one a Trinitarian in the technical sense of the term. The formula for the doctrine of the Trinity is specific: There is one God, and this one God is defined as a unity of three Persons.

While all Trinitarian churches hold to this core concept, within Trinitarianism there can be notable peripheral variation from one denomination to another. So to be clear, when I talk about the doctrine of the Trinity here, I am referring to the Seventh-day Adventist version of it as presented in our official publications.

---

140 *Ibid.*
141 *Seventh-day Adventist Church Manual,* 19th Edition, revised 2015, p. 162.

There is one God: Father, Son, and Holy Spirit, a unity of three co-eternal Persons. (Fundamental Belief #2)

Summary of Concerns

An analysis of the implications of this teaching brings up a number of deeper issues:

1. No author under inspiration, either a Bible writer or Ellen White, has ever officially defined "God" as a unity of three Persons.[142] As we have seen, whenever the Bible specifically indicates who the "one God" is, it is always the Father.[143] Ellen White rightly acknowledged the "three living persons of the heavenly trio,"[144] and in the process of doing so, she identified "God" as "the Father."[145] The point to notice here is that our doctrinal statement **differs materially from the explanation that Inspiration has provided**.

2. The enforcement of this formulation **imposes a man-made test**, something we have been clearly warned against.

    > The Lord does not require that any tests of human inventions shall be brought in to divert the minds of the people or create controversy in any line.[146]

    > Do not present theories or tests that Christ has never mentioned and that have no foundation in the Bible. We have grand, solemn truths to present. "It is written" is the test that must be brought home to every soul.[147]

---

142 "From my girlhood I have been given plain instruction that God is *a person*, and that Christ is 'the express image of His person' " (Ellen G. White Manuscript 137, 1903).

143 1 Corinthians 8:6; Ephesians 4:6; 1 Timothy 2:5.

144 *Evangelism*, p. 615.

145 *Ibid.*, p. 614, par. 3.

146 *Selected Messages*, Book Three, p. 252.

147 *Testimonies for the Church*, vol. 8, p. 300.

3. Although the Old Testament speaks of God as having a Son long before Jesus ever took on humanity,[148] Adventist publications have denied that Jesus was originally, inherently God's Son in any true sense.[149] This denial **places the Seventh-day Adventist Church on the wrong side of the controversy in heaven** before the expulsion of Satan.

> Well, Lucifer, he was striving; he had glory in the heavenly courts, but he was striving for Christ's place next to God. Next he wanted to be God, but he could not obtain that.
> *Christ was the only begotten Son of God*, and Lucifer, that glorious angel, *got up a warfare over the matter*, until he had to be thrust down to the earth.[150]

Yes, there was a controversy over Christ's Sonship. While "angels that were loyal and true" "*clearly* set forth that Jesus was the Son of God,"[151] "this fact the [fallen] angels would *obscure*, that Christ was the only begotten Son of God."[152]

In light of that underlying conflict, it is remarkable that the *one* basic and essential confession of faith in the New Testament—Jesus is the Son of God—is not once acknowledged in the Fundamental Beliefs of Seventh-day Adventists.

4. The doctrine of the Trinity struggles when it comes to defending the singularity of God.[153] Theologians teach that each member of the Trinity is self-existent, not dependent

---

148 Proverbs 30:4; Daniel 3:25.

149 *Ministry*, June 1982, p. 24; *Adventist Review*, October 31, 1996, p. 12; etc.

150 White, 25LtMs, Ms 86, 1910, par. 28, 29.

151 White, *The Spirit of Prophecy*, Vol. 1, p. 19.

152 *This Day With God*, p. 128.

153 "How Father, Son, and Holy Spirit are three distinct personalities and yet one, how they are equal in power and authority and yet one, is beyond logic and reason" (J. R. Spangler, *Review and Herald*, October 21, 1971, p. 7).

on any other divine being for His existence.[154] More than just separate persons, that would make three independent sources of life. It is believed that Jesus' life is distinctly His own, separate from that of the Father. The Holy Spirit's life is distinct from that of the Father and the Son. Thus they may all have the same kind of life, but because of their independent self-existence, they each have their own separate life. Their oneness is viewed as "a unity of relationship, not necessarily a numerical or mathematical oneness."[155] They are one in character and purpose, but not in number. The problem here is that if each has a distinct, self-existent life, then by actual count we have three Gods.[156] To the rational mind, this **is indistinguishable from tritheism.**[157]

5. At the heart of this issue is the question of whether or not the divine Persons are one in essence. To properly understand this, we need to go back to the fourth century debates. The Council of Nicaea (AD 325) convened to address the challenge introduced by Arius to the general understanding of the church at that time as defended by Alexander.

> It appears that with the exception of a single point, the two views were identical, only being stated in different ways. The single point where the difference lay was that Alexander held that the Son was begotten of the *very essence* of the Father, and is therefore of the *same substance*

---

154 Whidden, Moon, Reeve, *The Trinity: Understanding God's Love, His Plan of Salvation, and Christian Relationships*, Review and Herald Publishing Association, 2002, p. 19.

155 Paul Petersen, "Trinity in the Bible," Part I, *Elder's Digest*, Oct/Dec 2010, pp. 23-25.

156 These are enumerated in the *Fundamental Beliefs of Seventh-day Adventists* as "God the eternal Father," "God the eternal Son," and "God the eternal Spirit."

157 Kwabena Donkor, *God in 3 Persons—In Theology*, Biblical Research Institute Release-9, pp. 25, 26.

with the Father, while Arius held that the Son was begotten by the Father, not from his own essence, but from
nothing; but that when he was thus begotten, he was, and
is, of precisely the *like substance* with the Father.

Whether the Son of God, therefore, is of the *same* substance, or only of *like* substance, with the Father, was the
question in dispute.[158]

Arius "asserted that…the Son is *essentially distinct* from the
Father."[159]

In condemning Arius and his position, the council hoped
to forever settle the matter. But as the problem did not go
away, one council after another was held, with decisions
going back and forth. The Council of Constantinople (AD
381) produced the final word on the matter, which would
be enforced from that point on.

The Cappadocians—Basil the Great, Gregory of Nyssa, and
Gregory of Nazianzus—used the Greek word *ousia* ("essence") to clarify what unifies the divine Persons. They understood this term as synonymous with Tertullian's earlier
use of the Latin term *substantia* ("substance").[160] The Greek
term *homoousios* ("same essence") became the basis for the
Latin term *consubstantialis*, or in English, *consubstantial* ("of
the same substance or essence"). This concept summarizes
the Nicene-Constantinopolitan explanation of the oneness
of God. And because, to the Catholic mind, the Father
is ungenerated and the Son is generated, shared essence
would mean that the Son is begotten of the substance or
essence of the Father.

---

158 Alonzo T. Jones, *The Two Republics*, pp. 333, 334, emphasis his.
159 Philip Schaff, *History of the Christian Church*, Vol. 3, (5th ed.; New York:
      Scribner. 1902) §124, "Arianism," p. 646.
160 Donkor, p. 11.

Arius rejected that explanation of the divine oneness, stating that Jesus' substance or essence, though it was like that of the Father, was separate and distinct from the Father. When combined with the idea of "generation" or "begottenness," Arius' view equates to a created Son, for creation is when something comes forth *from nothing*. The orthodox view, however, although it retains the concept of "generation," is able to avoid the conclusion of createdness by its insistence on oneness of essence.

So, where does the Adventist doctrine fit into this?

> The Adventist doctrine of the Trinity is not, theologically, identical with the traditional Christian doctrine. Adventists, therefore, subscribe to the ecumenical creeds on this doctrine only in their basic affirmation of the triune God, but not to its traditional Christian interpretation.[161]

Although Adventist authors at times employ the classical terminology of "one substance,"[162] it is not intended to mean the same thing that it meant in the classical tradition. The Adventist position does not formally address, ontologically, *how* the Father, Son, and Holy Spirit are one.

> When Adventists affirm that God is one they mean something different than what the tradition affirms. Without a burden to define rationally God's oneness, Adventists are uncomfortable with interpreting or defining it with reference to *substance* in such terms as simplicity, un-differentiation, etc.[163]

161 *Ibid.*, pp. 22, 23.
162 "The Doctrine of the Trinity Among Adventists," Gerhard Pfandl, Biblical Research Institute, June 1999, p. 1; "Reflections on the Doctrine of the Trinity," Raoul Dederen, *Andrews University Seminary Studies*, Vol. 8, 1970, No. 1.
163 Donkor, p. 23.

Consequently, the indivisibility of God's works in history is not conceived by Adventists as being determined by the oneness of essence—as taught by the Augustinian classical tradition—but rather by the oneness of the historical task of redemption.[164]

This is where the Adventist view starts looking like tritheism.

The danger of Tritheism involved in this position becomes real when the oneness of God is reduced to a mere unity conceived in analogy to a human society or a fellowship of action.[165]

The tradition read about the oneness of God in Scripture, defined it as *ousia*, and worked out an explanation of the three Persons accordingly. The issue is how one may *define* the "One" and relate it to the three Persons without falling into tritheism. It may be that theology needs to acknowledge its impotence in this matter.[166]

Rejecting the Greek concept of "generation" in relation to Christ, we, as a denomination, have avoided the heretical belief that Jesus was created. But in terms of the central issue in the historic debate—oneness of essence—Adventist Trinitarianism, by denying the Nicene affirmation regarding "Jesus Christ, the Son of God, *begotten of the Father*, only begotten that is to say, *of the substance of the Father*,"[167] **more closely aligns the Seventh-day Adventist Church with Arius** who contended that Jesus "does not derive His subsistence from any matter; but that by His own

---

164 Fernando Canale, "Doctrine of God," *Handbook of Seventh-day Adventist Theology*, p. 150.

165 *Ibid.*

166 Donkor. p. 26, emphasis his.

167 Arthur Penrhyn Stanley, *Lectures on the History of the Eastern Church*, p. 163.

will and counsel He has subsisted before time, and before ages, as perfect God."[168]

6. Because Christ's divine life is viewed as distinct from that of the Father, the Adventist position **requires us to distinguish between Christ's divine life and His human life**. Bible verses such as John 5:26 that don't fit into our conception of His divine life, are for that reason consigned to His human life.[169] The interpretation of "original, unborrowed, underived,"[170] so often applied to His divine life, notably excludes His human life.[171] And because His divinity could not die,[172] once we assign to Jesus a divinity independent of the Father, we are forced to view Him as having, almost in a dualistic sense, two separate lives, one that died, and one that did not. But Inspiration gives no hint of dualism. Jesus had but one life. "A divine spirit dwelt in a temple of flesh."[173]

7. As mentioned in the previous point, the doctrine of the Trinity **leads to the conclusion that Jesus did not completely die**. The human side of Jesus died. But His divine side only "as good as died."[174] In a Trinitarian view of the atonement, the Second Person of the Trinity acquires a human version of Himself that is capable of bearing the death penalty for sin, while His original, divine life survives

---

168 *The Ecclesiastical History of Theodoret*, Book I, Chapter V, p. 24.

169 "Remember this [John 5:26] refers to Jesus in His incarnation 'because he is the Son of man' (5:27)." –Gerhard Pfandl to the author, March 13, 2013.

170 *The Desire of Ages*, p. 530.

171 "It is significant that she [in 1SM 296] starts off with John 1:1 because there she speaks about the eternal divinity of Christ and only in this context can it be true that 'in Him was life, original, unborrowed, underived.'" –Gerhard Pfandl to the author, March 13, 2013.

172 "Humanity died; divinity did not die" (*Selected Messages*, Book One, p. 301).

173 White, "Christ's Humiliation," *The Youth's Instructor*, December 20, 1900, par. 7.

174 Whidden et al., p. 249, par. 6.

and, according to some accounts, resurrects His human life on Sunday morning. When you assign to Jesus a divine life that is distinct from that of the Father, and then differentiate His divine life from the human life He sacrificed, you end up with a Savior who didn't *fully* die on the cross.

8. The Trinitarian view of the atonement **makes the Father's participation only indirect and vicarious**. He looked on, and then turned His back, as His partner was tortured to death; but He Himself did not personally bear our punishment, because His life is distinct from Christ's. Ellen White, however, presents Christ's sacrifice as the Father giving *Himself*.[175] That point is lost in the prevailing model where each Person of the Trinity has His own independent life.[176]

9. Seventh-day Adventists currently teach that there was a time when one Person of the Godhead was "installed into a mediatorial role" "to become the Mediator."[177] In other words, Jesus was not originally, inherently the Mediator, but He took on that role at some point in time. This view, required by the doctrine of the Trinity, turns out just as Bible prophecy predicted. In fulfillment of Daniel 12:11, the AD 508 military triumph of Trinitarianism[178] **takes away**

---

175 *Steps to Christ*, p. 54; *Christ's Object Lessons*, pp. 174, 191.

176 Woodrow Whidden says, "Because of their profound unity of triune oneness in nature, we can acknowledge that the Father and the Holy Spirit were also profoundly present and in solidarity with Christ's atoning death" (*The Trinity*, p. 266). But that falls short of the Father's actual "sacrifice of Himself. He gave Himself in His Son." (White, *Australasian Union Conference Record*, June 1, 1900, Art. A, par. 11). "God Himself was crucified with Christ; for Christ was one with the Father" (White, *The Faith I Live By*, p. 50).

177 Richard M. Davidson, "Proverbs 8 and the Place of Christ in the Trinity," *Journal of the Adventist Theological Society*, 17/1 (Spring 2006), pp. 54, 53.

178 William H. Shea has recognized Clovis' defeat of the Visigoths as "a theological victory for the bishop of Rome" (*The Abundant Life Bible Amplifier: Daniel*

the *tamid*—"continual, always, ever, perpetual"—aspect of Jesus' mediatorial position.

10. Fundamental Belief #2, if I may borrow Ellen White's description of an approaching danger,[179] is a doctrine that **denies the past experience of the people of God**, evidence of a system of intellectual philosophy in which the fundamental principles that sustained the work for fifty years are now accounted as error.

A Simple Fix

These difficulties all result from our efforts to formulate a statement that goes beyond what the apostles and prophets have written.

The inspired explanation is simple: "Through the beloved Son, the Father's life flows out to all."[180] Since Jesus' life is actually His Father's, it is neither a separate divinity nor an inferior derivative. It is the very life of God, bearing all the Father's authority, power, honor and glory. That divine life, neither generated nor created, has eternally existed.

While those who attempt to explain exactly *how* Jesus is God's Son are treading on forbidden ground, those who *deny* His true Sonship by relegating it to the category of metaphor are taking away the only explanation of Jesus' divinity that is consistent with all the revealed data. Only *as the Son of God* could Jesus be equal with God and yet not be another God. Only as the Son of God is Jesus the Divine Sacrifice for sin.

> The cross! the cross! it is set up that we may understand
> and know the only true God, and Jesus Christ whom He

7-12, Pacific Press, 1996, p. 220).
179 *Selected Messages*, Book One, p. 204.
180 *The Desire of Ages*, p. 21.

has sent. It tells us of the depth and breadth of infinite love, the greatness of the Father's love. It reveals the astonishing truth that *God the Father gave Himself in His Son*, that He might have the joy of receiving back the sheep that was lost.[181]

All things come of God. From the smallest benefits up to the largest blessing, all flow through the one Channel—a superhuman mediation sprinkled with the blood that is of value beyond estimate because *it was the life of God in His Son*.[182]

Laying aside all forced interpretations, we will find at the conclusion of an honest inquiry that the truth is exactly as the Bible presents it. We need not attempt to improve on it.

---

181 *Manuscript Releases*, Vol. 17, p. 214.
182 *Faith and Works*, p. 22.

NO OTHER WAY

"For I delivered unto you first of all that which I also received, how that *Christ died for our sins* according to the scriptures."[183]

"The mystery of the cross explains all other mysteries."[184]

With its predominant emphasis on the *threefold* nature of the Godhead, Adventist Trinitarianism admittedly finds it difficult to meaningfully defend the oneness of God.[185] Dismissing as metaphorical[186] the biblical expressions establishing a basis for real, substantive oneness, our current theology is able only to explain it as a mysterious unity of purpose and action among three equals:

> The indivisibility of God's works in history is not conceived by Adventists as being determined by the oneness of *essence*—as taught by the Augustinian classical tradition—but rather by the oneness of the historical *task of redemption*.[187]

What the notion of a triune (group) God seems to suggest

---

183 1 Corinthians 15:3.

184 *The Great Controversy*, p. 652.

185 Donkor, p. 26.

186 "The Father-Son relationship in the Godhead should be understood in a metaphorical sense, not in a literal sense" (Max Hatton, *Understanding the Trinity*, p. 97).

187 Fernando Canale, "Doctrine of God," in Raoul Dederen, ed., *Handbook of Seventh-day Adventist Theology*, p. 150.

is that the three members of the Godhead become joined in their relationship with each other, on the basis of their common *purpose, values and interests*.[188]

The Spirit of Prophecy, however, presents a clearer explanation of the divine oneness, and, in so doing, settles the famous fourth-century debate:[189]

> The words of Christ were full of deep meaning as he put forth the claim that he and the Father were of *one substance*.[190]

As we have seen, when you eliminate *essential* oneness, you are left with the coexistence of multiple divine lives. Not only is this, in all practical terms, indistinguishable from tritheism, but it also poses another challenge. How does one who by nature is independently self-existent *die*?

Here is the difficulty Trinitarianism poses to the Atonement: Because divinity cannot die, if there are three self-existent divine lives, it could not be the divine side of Christ that died, but only the human part formed in Mary's womb. His original divine life would remain untouched. In that case, none of the three divine lives, as they originally existed, actually died.

This would mean that the inherent life of the second Person of the Trinity was never in jeopardy. He faced no real, eternal risk to His life. But Inspiration asserts just the opposite:

> Remember that Christ risked all; "tempted like as we are," he staked even his own eternal existence upon the issue of

---

188 Lionel Matthews, Ph.D., Andrews University, *Sociology: A Biblical Perspective*, 3rd Symposium on the Bible and Adventist Scholarship, General Conference Education Department, 2006, p. 11.

189 *Homoousios* (*same* substance or essence) vs. *homoiousios* (*similar* substance or essence).

190 White, *Signs of the Times*, November 27, 1893.

the conflict.[191]

> To the honor and glory of God, His beloved Son—the Surety, the Substitute—was delivered up and descended into the prisonhouse of the grave. The new tomb enclosed Him in its rocky chambers. If one single sin had tainted His character *the stone would never have been rolled away from the door of His rocky chamber*, and the world with its burden of guilt would have perished.[192]

Let's explore a little deeper this question of Jesus' ability to die. If Jesus had His own, exclusive, personal divine life, His mortal humanity would need to be detached from His immortal divinity in order to be able to die on the cross. But this would defeat the whole purpose of the Incarnation. The Incarnation is the key to the Atonement. It wasn't just about Jesus becoming human. In the Incarnation, divinity was *vitally combined with* humanity.

> Divinity and humanity were mysteriously *combined*, and man and God became one. It is *in this union* that we find the hope of our fallen race.[193]

> The two natures were mysteriously *blended* in one person—the man Christ Jesus.[194]

It is that *blending* of the two natures that makes His death efficacious. But if that union is broken, it negates the whole effect of the Incarnation. Humanity would be severed from divinity, leaving no hope for the fallen race.

> *In taking our nature*, the Saviour has bound Himself to humanity by a tie that is *never to be broken....* God gave His

---

191 *General Conference Bulletin*, December 1, 1895, Art. B, par. 23.
192 *Manuscript Releases*, Vol. 10, p. 385.1 (Manuscript 81, 1893).
193 White, *Signs of the Times,* July 30, 1896.
194 White, *SDA Bible Commentary,* Vol., 5, p. 1113.

only-begotten Son to become one of the human family, *forever to retain His human nature.*[195]

Christ's humanity *could not be separated* from His divinity.[196]

How, then, could He die? Jesus provides the definitive answer in His words, "I live by the Father." John 6:57.

He declared that he had no existence separate from the Father.[197]

And when Jesus had cried with a loud voice, he said, Father, into thy hands I commend my spirit: and having said thus, he gave up the ghost. (Luke 23:46)

The spirit shall return unto God who gave it. (Ecclesiastes 12:7)

"Because it was the life of God in His Son,"[198] and because He had no other life of His own, Jesus could truly die, and pay the complete price for our redemption.

But if the immortal divine life that He possessed had been uniquely and exclusively His own, He could not have truly died.

God has given in His word *decisive evidence* that He will punish the transgressors of His law. Those who flatter themselves that He is too merciful to execute justice upon the sinner, have only to look to the cross of Calvary. *The death of the spotless Son of God testifies that "the wages of sin is death,"* that every violation of God's law must receive its

---

195 *The Desire of Ages*, p. 25.
196 White, *Signs of the Times*, April 14, 1898.
197 White, *Review and Herald*, January 7, 1890.
198 *Faith and Works*, p. 22.

just retribution.[199]

Let's make sure we grasp this point in its context. This is the chapter in *The Great Controversy* entitled, "The First Great Deception." Satan's lie in the garden was, "Ye shall not surely die." Here Sister White is presenting absolute proof that the wages of sin is death. She contends that the death of Christ provides the "decisive evidence." But, if He who was in the beginning with God did not *surely* die, then the wages of sin is not death, and Satan's assertion in the garden was true.

But Jesus *did* completely give up His life:

> Christ the sinless became sin for man. He bore the guilt of transgression, and the hiding of His Father's face, until His heart was broken and *His life crushed out.* All this sacrifice was made that sinners might be redeemed. *In no other way* could man be freed from the penalty of sin. And every soul that refuses to become a partaker of the atonement provided at *such a cost* must bear in his own person the guilt and punishment of transgression.[200]

> He laid down his life for us. (1 John 3:16)

> The plan of redemption will not be fully understood, even when the ransomed see as they are seen and know as they are known; but through the eternal ages new truth will continually unfold to the wondering and delighted mind. Though the griefs and pains and temptations of earth are ended and the cause removed, the people of God will ever have a distinct, intelligent knowledge of *what their salvation has cost.*
>
> The cross of Christ will be the science and the song of the redeemed through all eternity. In Christ glorified they will behold Christ crucified. Never will it be forgotten

---

199 *The Great Controversy*, pp. 539, 540.
200 *Ibid.*, p. 540.

that He whose power created and upheld the unnumbered worlds through the vast realms of space, the Beloved of God, the Majesty of heaven, He whom cherub and shining seraph delighted to adore—humbled Himself to uplift fallen man; that *He bore the guilt and shame of sin,* and the hiding of His Father's face, till the woes of a lost world broke His heart and *crushed out His life* on Calvary's cross.[201]

It will be seen that He who is infinite in wisdom could devise no plan for our salvation except the sacrifice of His Son.[202]

---

201 *Ibid.,* p. 651.
202 *Ibid.,* p. 652.

FATHER, SON, AND HOLY SPIRIT

One God, the Father

"But unto us there is but one God, the Father, of whom are all things, and we in him; and one Lord Jesus Christ, by whom are all things, and we by him." 1 Corinthians 8:6

"From my girlhood I have been given plain instruction that God is a person, and that Christ is 'the express image of His person.' " Ms 137, 1903

"For there is one God, and one mediator between God and men, the man Christ Jesus." 1 Timothy 2:5

"In His prayer to the Father, Christ gave to the world a lesson which should be graven on mind and soul. 'This is life eternal,' He said, 'that they might know Thee the only true God, and Jesus Christ, whom Thou hast sent.' John 17:3." COL 114

"To serve the living and true God; And to wait for his Son" 1 Thessalonians 1:9, 10

"One God and Father of all, who is above all, and through all, and in you all." Ephesians 4:6

"Him which is, and which was, and which is to come" Revelation 1:4

"The great Eternal" 2SP 85

"The Sovereign of the universe" PP 34

"The Ruler of all things" RH April 18, 1893

"The Majesty on high" Hebrews 1:3

"Lord of heaven and earth" Matthew 11:25

"The Ancient of days" Daniel 7:9

"The Ancient of days is God the Father. Says the psalmist, 'Before the mountains were brought forth,

95

or ever Thou hadst formed the earth and the world, even from everlasting to everlasting, Thou art God.' Psalm 90:2. It is He, the source of all being, and the fountain of all law, that is to preside in the judgment." GC 479

"Our Father in heaven is the source of life, of wisdom, and of joy." SC 9

"God is the fountain of life, and we can have life only as we are in communion with Him. Separated from God, existence may be ours for a little time, but we do not possess life…. Only through the surrender of our will to God is it possible for Him to impart life to us. Only by receiving His life through self-surrender is it possible, said Jesus, for these hidden sins, which I have pointed out, to be overcome." MB 61

"For this cause I bow my knees unto the Father of our Lord Jesus Christ, of whom the whole family in heaven and earth is named." Ephesians 3:14, 15

"Blessed be the God and Father of our Lord Jesus Christ." 1 Peter 1:3

"The God of our Lord Jesus Christ, the Father of glory" Ephesians 1:17

"Jesus saith unto her,… I ascend unto my Father, and your Father;

and to my God, and your God." John 20:17

"Now unto the King eternal, immortal, invisible, the only wise God, be honour and glory for ever and ever. Amen." 1 Timothy 1:17

"Who only hath immortality, dwelling in the light which no man can approach unto; whom no man hath seen, nor can see: to whom be honour and power everlasting. Amen." 1 Timothy 6:16

"The Father's person I could not behold, for a cloud of glorious light covered Him. I asked Jesus if His Father had a form like Himself. He said He had, but I could not behold it, for said He, 'If you should once behold the glory of His person, you would cease to exist.'" EW 54

"I asked Him if His Father was a person and had a form like Himself. Said Jesus, 'I am in the express image of My Father's person.'" EW 77

"Through Jesus Christ, God—not a perfume, not something intangible, but a personal God—created man, and endowed him with intelligence and power." 3MR 355

"No man hath seen God at any time; the only begotten Son, which is in the bosom of the Father, he hath declared him." John 1:18

Jesus Christ, the Son of God

"Jesus Christ, the Son of God" Mark 1:1

"God is the Father of Christ; Christ is the Son of God." 8T 268

"The Son of the infinite God" TM 220

"The Son of the Eternal" DA 112

"The only begotten Son of God" John 3:18

"The only begotten of the Father" John 1:14

"God sent his only begotten Son." 1 John 4:9

"Thy holy child Jesus" Acts 4:27, 30

" 'He gave his only-begotten Son,'—not a son by creation, as were the angels, nor a son by adoption, as is the forgiven sinner, but a Son begotten in the express image of the Father's person, and in all the brightness of his majesty and glory, one equal with God in authority, dignity, and divine perfection. In him dwelt all the fullness of the Godhead bodily." ST May 30, 1895

" 'Wist ye not,' He said, 'that I must be about my Father's business?'... In the answer to His mother, Jesus showed for the first time that He understood His relation to God." DA 81

"He had...declared His Sonship to God." DA 82

"My Father worketh hitherto, and I work. Therefore the Jews sought the more to kill him, because he... said...that God was his Father, making himself equal with God." John 5:17, 18

"Jesus...in calling God 'His own Father' had declared Himself equal with God." DA 207

"The whole nation of the Jews called God their Father, therefore they would not have been so enraged if Christ had represented Himself as standing in the same relation to God. But they accused Him of blasphemy, showing that they understood Him as making this claim in the highest sense." DA 207, 208

"In this discourse He fully explained to them His Sonship, the relation He bore to the Father and His equality with Him." 2SP 172

"The god of this world hath blinded the minds of them which believe not, lest the light of the glorious gospel of Christ, who is the image of God, should shine unto them." 2 Corinthians 4:4

"Who is the image of the invisible God, the firstborn of every creature." Colossians 1:15

"The dedication of the first-born had its origin in the earliest times. God had promised to give the First-born of heaven to save the sinner." DA 51

"The First begotten of God" UL 357

"Whose goings forth have been from of old, from everlasting." Micah 5:2

"Who had dwelt in the innermost sanctuary of the Eternal." COL 38

"I came out from God. I came forth from the Father." John 16:27, 28

"And have known surely that I came out from thee." John 17:8

"I proceeded forth and came from God." John 8:42

"Through Solomon Christ declared: 'The Lord possessed Me in the beginning of His way.'" ST August 29, 1900

" 'The Lord possessed me in the beginning of his way,' He declares, 'before his works of old. I was set up from everlasting, from the

beginning, or ever the earth was. When there were no depths, I was brought forth; when there were no fountains abounding with water. Before the mountains were settled, before the hills was I brought forth: while as yet he had not made the earth, nor the fields, nor the highest part of the dust of the world. When he prepared the heavens, I was there: when he set a compass upon the face of the depth' (Prov. 8:22-27)." 1SM 248

"The Scriptures clearly indicate the relation between God and Christ, and they bring to view as clearly the personality and individuality of each. 'God...hath in these last days spoken unto us by His Son, whom He hath appointed heir of all things, by whom also He made the worlds; who being the brightness of His glory, and the express image of His person, and upholding all things by the word of His power, when He had by Himself purged our sins, sat down on the right hand of the Majesty on high; being made so much better than the angels, as He hath by inheritance obtained a more excellent name than they. For unto which of the angels said He at any time, Thou art My Son, this day have I begotten Thee? And again, I will be to Him a Father, and He shall be to me a Son?' Hebrews 1:1-5." 8T 268

"And again, when he bringeth in the firstbegotten into the world, he saith, And let all the angels of God worship him. And of the angels he saith, Who maketh his angels spirits, and his ministers a flame of fire. But unto the Son he saith, Thy throne, O God, is for ever and ever: a sceptre of righteousness is the sceptre of thy kingdom. Thou hast loved righteousness, and hated iniquity; therefore God, even thy God, hath anointed thee with the oil of gladness above thy fellows. And, Thou, Lord, in the beginning hast laid the foundation of the earth; and the heavens are the works of thine hands: They shall perish; but thou remainest; and they all shall wax old as doth a garment; And as a vesture shalt thou fold them up, and they shall be changed: but thou art the same, and thy years shall not fail." Hebrews 1:6-12

"In reality He was the Son of the infinite God." CTr 227

"Wherefore God also hath highly exalted him, and given him a name which is above every name: That at the name of Jesus every knee should bow, of things in heaven, and things in earth, and things under the earth; And that every tongue should confess that Jesus Christ is Lord, to the glory of God the Father." Philippians 2:9-11

"We do believe in the divinity of Christ and in His preexistence." TM 253

"The divinity of Christ is the believer's assurance of eternal life." DA 530

"In the beginning was the Word, and the Word was with God, and the Word was God. The same was in the beginning with God. All things were made by him; and without him was not any thing made that was made." John 1:1-3

"The Father wrought by His Son in the creation of all heavenly beings." PP 34

"For by him were all things created, that are in heaven, and that are in earth, visible and invisible, whether they be thrones, or dominions, or principalities, or powers: all things were created by him, and for him: And he is before all things, and by him all things consist." Colossians 1:16, 17

"In him was life; and the life was the light of men." John 1:4

"In Christ is life, original, unborrowed, underived." DA 530

"In Him is gathered all the glory of the Father, the fullness of the Godhead. He is the brightness of the Father's glory and the express image of His person." COL 115

"God hath given to us eternal life, and this life is in his Son. He that hath the Son hath life; and he that hath not the Son of God hath not life." 1 John 5:11, 12

"For as the Father hath life in himself; so hath he given to the Son to have life in himself." John 5:26

"For it pleased the Father that in him should all fulness dwell." Colossians 1:19

"God has sent his Son to communicate his own life to humanity. Christ declares, 'I live by the Father,' my life and his being one." HM June 1, 1897

"He declared that He had no existence separate from the Father." RH January 7, 1890

"Jesus said, 'I and my Father are one.' The words of Christ were full of deep meaning as He put forth the claim that He and the Father were of one substance, possessing the same attributes." ST November 27, 1893

"All things Christ received from God, but He took to give. So in the heavenly courts, in His ministry for all created beings: through the beloved Son, the Father's life flows out to all; through the Son it returns, in praise and joyous service, a tide of love, to the great Source of all." DA 21

"All things come of God. From the smallest benefits up to the largest blessing, all flow through one Channel—a superhuman mediation sprinkled with the blood that is of value beyond estimate because it was the life of God in His Son." FW 22

"God offered them, in His Son, the perfect righteousness of the law. If they would open their hearts fully to receive Christ, then the very life of God, His love, would dwell in them." MB 55

"God could not express greater love than He has expressed in giving the Son of His bosom to this world." OHC 13

"The Eternal Father, the unchangeable one, gave his only begotten Son, tore from his bosom Him who was made in the express image of his person, and sent him down to earth to reveal how greatly he loved mankind." RH July 9, 1895

"God's love for the world was not manifest because He sent His Son, but because He loved the world He sent His Son into the world that divinity clothed with humanity might touch humanity, while divinity lays hold of divinity. Though sin had produced a gulf between man and his God, a divine benevolence provided a plan to bridge that gulf. And what material did He use? A part of Himself. The brightness of the Father's glory came to a world all seared and marred with the curse, and in His own divine character, in His own divine body, bridged the gulf." OHC 12

"God was in Christ, reconciling the world unto himself." 2 Corinthians 5:19

"God gave Himself in His Son." COL 191

"In Christ was the embodiment of God himself." 3SP 186

"Our Saviour, the outshining of the Father's glory." COL 126

"What speech is to thought, so is Christ to the invisible Father. He is the manifestation of the Father, and is called the Word of God." TMK 38

"Christ the Word, the Only Begotten of God, was one with the eternal Father,—one in nature, in character, and in purpose,—the only being in all the universe that could enter into all the counsels and purposes of God." GC 493

"The Son of God shared the Father's throne, and the glory of the eternal, self-existent One encircled both." PP 36

"And the counsel of peace shall be between them both." Zechariah 6:13

"Before the assembled inhabitants of heaven the King declared that none but Christ, the Only Begotten of God, could fully enter into His purposes, and to Him it was committed to execute the mighty counsels of His will." PP 36

"To know God is to love Him; His character must be manifested in contrast to the character of Satan. This work only one Being in all the universe could do. Only He who knew the height and depth of the love of God could make it known. Upon the world's dark night the Sun of Righteousness must rise, 'with healing in His wings.' " DA 22

"The only Being who was one with God lived the law in humanity, descended to the lowly life of a common laborer, and toiled at the carpenter's bench with his earthly parent." TMK 363

"Lucifer in heaven, before his rebellion, was a high and exalted angel, next in honor to God's dear Son." SR 13

"Sin originated with him who, next to Christ, had been most honored of God and was highest in power and glory among the inhabitants of heaven." PP 35

"This fact the [fallen] angels would obscure, that Christ was the only begotten Son of God." TDG 128

"And Simon Peter answered and said, Thou art the Christ, the Son of the living God. And Jesus answered and said unto him, Blessed art thou, Simon Barjona: for flesh and blood hath not revealed it unto thee, but my Father which is in heaven." Matthew 16:16, 17

"The truth which Peter had confessed is the foundation of the believer's faith." DA 412

"Peter had expressed the truth which is the foundation of the church's faith." DA 413

"Whosoever shall confess that Jesus is the Son of God, God dwelleth in him, and he in God." 1 John 4:15

"Let the missionaries of the cross proclaim that there is one God, and one Mediator between God and man, who is Jesus Christ the Son of the Infinite God. This needs to be proclaimed throughout every church in our land. Christians need to know this." 1888 886

"Who is a liar but he that denieth that Jesus is the Christ? He is antichrist, that denieth the Father and the Son." 1 John 2:22

"Denying the only Lord God, and our Lord Jesus Christ." Jude 4

"But these are written, that ye might believe that Jesus is the Christ, the Son of God." John 20:31

"Through the grace of Christ every soul must work out his own righteousness, maintaining a living connection with the Father and the Son." TM 488

"And truly our fellowship is with the Father, and with his Son Jesus Christ." 1 John 1:3

"Grace be with you, mercy, and peace, from God the Father, and from the Lord Jesus Christ, the Son of the Father, in truth and love." 2 John 3

"Blessing, and honour, and glory, and power, be unto him that sitteth upon the throne, and unto the Lamb, for ever and ever." Revelation 5:13

"The Father and the Son alone are to be exalted." SD 58

"The glory of God and the Lamb floods the holy city with unfading light.... 'I saw no temple therein: for the Lord God Almighty and the Lamb are the temple of it.' Rev. 21:22. The people of God are privileged to hold open communion with the Father and the

Son.... And as the years of eternity roll, they will bring richer and more glorious revelations of God and of Christ." SR 432

"Then cometh the end, when he shall have delivered up the kingdom to God, even the Father; when he shall have put down all rule and all authority and power. For he must reign, till he hath put all enemies under his feet.... And when all things shall be subdued unto him, then shall the Son also himself be subject unto him that put all things under him, that God may be all in all." 1 Corinthians 15:24-28

The Holy Spirit of God

"The holy Spirit of God" Ephesians 4:30

"Whither shall I go from thy spirit? or whither shall I flee from thy presence?" Psalm 139:7

"The Holy Spirit is the vital presence of God." ST August 7, 1901

"The divine Spirit that the world's Redeemer promised to send is the presence and power of God." YRP 39

"In the inner sanctuary of the soul the presence of God is to abide." YRP 42

"The Bible shows us God in His high and holy place, not in a state of inactivity, not in silence and solitude, but surrounded by ten thousand times ten thousand and thousands of thousands of holy beings, all waiting to do His will. Through these messengers He is in active communication with every part of His dominion. By His Spirit He is everywhere present. Through the agency of His Spirit and His angels He ministers to the children of men." MH 417

"The children of earth, who need so much the help that God only can give, seem satisfied to walk without the light of His Spirit, the companionship of His presence." SC 94

"Cast me not away from thy presence; and take not thy holy spirit from me." Psalm 51:11

"You need the Holy Spirit of God, the divine power." UL 101

"The prince of the power of evil can only be held in check by the power of God in the third person of the Godhead, the Holy Spirit." Ev 617

"The Spirit of your Father" Matthew 10:20

"The life-giving Spirit, flowing from the infinite fullness of God" DA 386

"Never before had angels listened to such a prayer as Christ offered at His baptism, and they were solicitous to be the bearers of the message from the Father to His Son. But, no! Direct from the Father issues the light of His glory. The heavens were opened and beams of glory rested upon the Son of God and assumed the form of a dove, in appearance like burnished gold. The dovelike form was emblematical of the meekness and gentleness of Christ." TMK 31

"It is by the Spirit that God works upon the heart; when men willfully reject the Spirit, and declare It to be from Satan, they cut off the channel by which God can communicate with them." DA 322

"If ye, then, being human and evil, 'know how to give good gifts unto your children: how much more shall your heavenly Father give the Holy Spirit to them that ask Him?' Luke 11:13. The Holy Spirit, the representative of Himself, is the greatest of all gifts." MB 132

"In giving us His Spirit, God gives us Himself, making Himself a fountain of divine influences, to give health and life to the world." 7T 273

"So the life-giving power of the Holy Spirit, proceeding from Christ, and imparted to every disciple, pervades the soul." LP 131

"The Holy Spirit is a person." Ev 616

"Sin could be resisted and overcome only through the mighty agency of the third person of the Godhead, who would come with no modified energy, but in the fulness of divine power." RH May 19, 1904

"We need to realize that the Holy Spirit, who is as much a person as God is a person, is walking through these grounds." Ev 616

"As God hath said, I will dwell in them, and walk in them." 2 Corinthians 6:16

"The Holy Spirit has a personality, else He could not bear witness to our spirits and with our spirits that we are the children of God. He must also be a divine person, else He could not search out the secrets which lie hidden in the mind of God. 'For what man knoweth the things of a man, save the spirit of man which is in him? Even so the things of God knoweth no man, but the Spirit of God.' " Ev 617

"The Holy Spirit is the Comforter, in Christ's name. He personifies Christ, yet is a distinct personality. We may have the Holy Spirit if we ask for it and make it [a] habit to turn to and trust in God rather than in any finite human agent who may make mistakes." 20MR 324

"The Holy Spirit is a free, working, independent agency. The God of heaven uses His Spirit as it pleases Him; and human minds, human judgment, and human methods can no more set boundaries to its working, or prescribe the channel through which it shall operate, than they can say to the wind, 'I bid you to blow in a certain direction, and to conduct yourself in such and such a manner.' As the wind moves in its force, bending and breaking the lofty trees in its path, so the Holy Spirit influences human hearts, and no finite man can circumscribe its work." ST March 8, 1910

"The Holy Spirit has gone out into all the world; everywhere it is moving upon the hearts of men." COL 70

"The secret things belong unto the Lord our God: but those things which are revealed belong unto us and to our children for ever." Deuteronomy 29:29

"The incarnation of Christ, His divinity, His atonement, His wonderful life in heaven as our advocate, the office of the Holy Spirit—all these living, vital themes of Christianity are revealed from Genesis to Revelation." FE 385

"It is all-essential for the Christian to understand the meaning of the promise of the Holy Spirit just prior to the coming of our Lord Jesus the second time. Talk of it, pray for it, preach concerning it; for the Lord is more willing to give the Holy Spirit than parents are to give good gifts to their children." YRP 10

"It is not essential for us to be able to define just what the Holy Spirit is." AA 51

"The nature of the Holy Spirit is a mystery. Men cannot explain it, because the Lord has not revealed it to them.... Regarding such mysteries, which are too deep for human understanding, silence is golden." AA 52

"I knew that I must warn our brethren and sisters not to enter into controversy over the presence and personality of God." 1SM 203

"It introduces that which is nought but speculation in regard to the personality of God and where His presence is. No one on this earth has a right to speculate on this question." 1SM 202

"These theories were invented by men who had not learned the first great lesson, that God's Spirit and life are in His Word." YRP 127

"The creative energy that called the worlds into existence is in the word of God. This word imparts power; it begets life. Every command is a promise; accepted by the will, received into the soul, it brings with it the life of the Infinite One." Ed 126

"The life of Christ that gives life to the world is in His word." DA 390

"God's holy, educating Spirit is in His word." YRP 141

" 'As the living Father hath sent me,' He says, 'and I live by the Father: so he that eateth me, even he shall live by me.' 'It is the spirit that quickeneth; the flesh profiteth nothing: the words that I speak unto you, they are spirit, and they are life' (John 6:57, 63). Christ is not here referring to His doctrine, but to His person, the divinity of His character." 1SM 249

"The Spirit of life from God entered into them." Revelation 11:11

"The Spirit giveth life." 2 Corinthians 3:6

"The Spirit of God hath made me, and the breath of the Almighty hath given me life." Job 33:4

"By the word of the Lord were the heavens made; and all the host of them by the breath of his mouth." Psalm 33:6

"The breath of the Lord of hosts must enter into the lifeless bodies.... It will then be clearly seen that...spiritual life from heaven was breathed upon one who was dead in trespasses and sins, and he was quickened with spiritual life.... The breath of life must vivify the bodies.... The hope of the church is the vivifying influence of the Holy Spirit. The Lord must breathe upon the dry bones, that they may live. The Spirit of God, with its vivifying power, must be in every human agent.... Without the Holy Spirit, without the breath of God, there is torpidity of conscience, loss of spiritual life." YRP 45

"The Holy Spirit is the breath of spiritual life in the soul." DA 805

"The spirit of life from heaven seemed to be breathed upon the people." GC 223

"Like the wind, which is invisible, yet the effects of which are plainly seen and felt, is the Spirit of God in its work upon the human heart." SC 57

"As the wind bloweth whither it listeth, and we cannot tell whence it cometh or whither it goeth, so it is with the Spirit of God. We do not know through whom it will be manifested." 1MR 179

"A spirit hath not flesh and bones, as ye see me have." Luke 24:39

"The precious Spirit, which is light and life." 2SM 17

"I saw a throne, and on it sat the Father and the Son.... Those who were bowed before the throne would offer up their prayers and look to Jesus; then He would look to His Father, and appear to be pleading with Him. A light would come from the Father to the Son and from the Son to the praying company. Then I saw an exceeding bright light come from the Father to the Son, and from the Son it waved over the people.... Those who rose up with Jesus would send up their faith to Him in the holiest, and pray, 'My Father, give us Thy Spirit.' Then Jesus would breathe upon them the Holy Ghost. In that breath was light, power, and much love, joy, and peace." EW 54, 55

"The Spirit of grace" Hebrews 10:29

"The Spirit of truth" John 16:13

"The Spirit of inspiration" MB 49

"In the great and measureless gift of the Holy Spirit are contained all of heaven's resources." COL 419

"How God anointed Jesus of Nazareth with the Holy Ghost and with power: who went about doing good, and healing all that were oppressed of the devil; for God was with him." Acts 10:38

"The Spirit of the Lord is upon me." Luke 4:18

"The Father is in me, and I in him." John 10:38

"The Father's presence encircled Christ." MB 71

"And now, O Father, glorify thou me with thine own self with the glory which I had with thee before the world was." John 17:5

"Believest thou not that I am in the Father, and the Father in me? the words that I speak unto you I speak not of myself: but the Father that dwelleth in me, he doeth the works. Believe me that I am in the Father, and the Father in me." John 14:10, 11

"God in His Son" COL 215

"Know ye not that ye are the temple of God, and that the Spirit of God dwelleth in you?" 1 Corinthians 3:16

"I will put my spirit within you." Ezekiel 36:27

"The high and holy One who inhabiteth eternity will not put His

Holy Spirit into unclean vessels.... He gives His Spirit in proportion to the consecration and self-sacrifice manifested by those who engage in His work." RH May 20, 1890

"The measure of the Holy Spirit we receive will be proportioned to the measure of our desire and the faith exercised for it, and the use we shall make of the light and knowledge that shall be given to us. We shall be entrusted with the Holy Spirit according to our capacity to receive and our ability to impart it to others." YRP 67

"The Father gave His Spirit without measure to His Son, and we also may partake of its fullness." GC 477

"Even the Spirit of truth, which proceedeth from the Father." John 15:26

"The Spirit of the living God" 2 Corinthians 3:3

"The Spirit that dwells in Him" 7T 12

"For ye are the temple of the living God." 2 Corinthians 6:16

"But ye are not in the flesh, but in the Spirit, if so be that the Spirit of God dwell in you. Now if any man have not the Spirit of Christ, he is none of his." Romans 8:9

"The Spirit of life in Christ Jesus" Romans 8:2

"God hath sent forth the Spirit of his Son into your hearts." Galatians 4:6

"Until Christ be formed in you." Galatians 4:19

"Christ in you, the hope of glory" Colossians 1:27

"Christ liveth in me." Galatians 2:20

"And if Christ be in you, the body is dead because of sin; but the Spirit is life because of righteousness." Romans 8:10

"I bow my knees unto the Father...that he would grant you, according to the riches of his glory, to be strengthened with might by his Spirit in the inner man; That Christ may dwell in your hearts by faith." Ephesians 3:14, 16, 17

"For where two or three are gathered together in my name, there am I in the midst of them." Matthew 18:20

"And, lo, I am with you alway, even unto the end of the world." Matthew 28:20

"If any man hear my voice, and open the door, I will come in to him." Revelation 3:20

"By an agency as unseen as the wind, Christ is constantly working upon the heart." DA 172

"Christ Himself is the renewing power, working in and through every soldier by the agency of the Holy Spirit." YRP 183

"I wish to impress upon you the fact that those who have Jesus abiding in the heart by faith, have actually received the Holy Spirit." 14MR 71

"The Holy Spirit is the Spirit of Christ." 14MR 84

"The Spirit of Jesus Christ" Philippians 1:19

"We can no more repent without the Spirit of Christ than we can be pardoned without Christ." SC 26

"It is the virtue that goes forth from Christ. that leads to genuine repentance." SC 26

"It is the power of Christ that is drawing them." SC 27

"The influence of the Holy Spirit is the life of Christ in the soul." YRP 130

"The impartation of the Spirit is the impartation of the life of Christ." DA 805

"If we keep our minds stayed upon Christ, He will come unto us 'as the rain, as the latter and former rain unto the earth.' Hosea 6:3. As the Sun of Righteousness, He will arise upon us 'with healing in His wings.' " COL 67

"And I will pray the Father, and he shall give you another Comforter, that he may abide with you for ever." John 14:16

"Christ declared that after his ascension, he would send to his church, as his crowning gift, the Comforter, who was to take his place. This Comforter is the Holy Spirit—the soul of his life, the efficacy of his church, the light and life of the world. With his Spirit Christ sends a reconciling influence and a power that takes away sin." RH May 19, 1904

"Even the Spirit of truth; whom the world cannot receive, because it seeth him not, neither knoweth him: but ye know him; for he dwelleth with you, and shall be in you. I will not leave you comfortless: I will come to you. Yet a little while, and the world seeth me no more; but ye see me: because I live, ye shall live also. At that day ye shall know that I am in my Father, and ye in me, and I in you." John 14:17-20

"This refers to the omnipresence of the Spirit of Christ, called the Comforter." 14MR 179

"The Saviour is our Comforter. This I have proved Him to be." 8MR 49

"The enemy…has sought to shut Jesus from their view as the Comforter, as one who reproves, who warns, who admonishes them, saying, 'This is the way, walk ye in it.' " RH August 26, 1890

"We adore God for His wondrous love in giving us Jesus the Comforter." SD 124

"We want the Holy Spirit, which is Jesus Christ." Lt 66, 1894

"Let them study the seventeenth of John, and learn how to pray and how to live the prayer of Christ. He is the Comforter. He will abide in their hearts, making their joy full." RH January 27, 1903

"Christ not only gave Himself for but to His disciples. The record declares, 'He breathed on them, and saith unto them, Receive ye the Holy Ghost' (John 20:22). Jesus is waiting to breathe upon all His disciples, and give them the inspiration of His sanctifying Spirit, and transfuse the vital influence from Himself to His people…. Christ is to live in His human agents…. They must act with His Spirit that it may be no more they that live, but Christ that liveth in them." YRP 26

"In giving His commission to His followers, Christ did not tell them they would be left alone. He assured them that He would be near them. He spoke of His Omnipresence in a special way. Go to all nations, He said. Go, to the farthest portion of the habitable globe, but know that My presence will be there. Labor in faith and confidence, for the time will never come when I shall forsake you." MS 138, 1897

"I will be with you always, helping you to perform your duty, guiding, comforting, sanctifying, sustaining you, giving you success in speaking words that shall draw the attention of others to heaven." AA 29

"All professions of Christianity are but lifeless expressions of faith until Jesus imbues the believer with his spiritual life, which is the Holy Ghost." 3SP 242

"Cumbered with humanity, Christ could not be in every place personally; therefore it was altogether for their advantage that He should leave them, go to His Father, and send the Holy Spirit to be His successor on earth. The Holy Spirit is Himself, divested of the personality of humanity, and independent thereof. He would represent Himself as present in all places by His Holy Spirit, as the Omnipresent." Lt 119, 1895, par. 18

"He comes personally by His Holy Spirit into the midst of His church." CET 206

"Jesus is seeking to impress upon them the thought that in giving His Holy Spirit He is giving to them the glory which the Father has given Him, that He and His people may be one in God." YRP 26

"In that day the redeemed will shine forth in the glory of the Father and His Son." Mar 39

"The pure, exalted, transporting glory that emanates from God and the Lamb." Mar 46

"If a man love me, he will keep my words: and my Father will love him, and we will come unto him, and make our abode with him." John 14:23

"That ye might be filled with all the fulness of God." Ephesians 3:19

"That they all may be one; as thou, Father, art in me, and I in thee, that they also may be one in us: that the world may believe that thou hast sent me. And the glory which thou gavest me I have given them; that they may be one, even as we are one: I in them, and thou in me, that they may be made perfect in one." John 17:21-23

"It is the Holy Spirit, the redeeming grace of truth in the soul, that makes the followers of Christ one with one another and one with God." YRP 34

"Christ, the true foundation, is a living stone; His life is imparted to all that are built upon Him. 'Ye also, as living stones, are built up a spiritual house.' 'Each several building, fitly framed together, groweth into a holy temple in the Lord.' 1 Peter 2:5, R.V.; Ephesians 2:21, R.V. The stones became one with the foundation; for a common life dwells in all. That building no tempest can overthrow; for—'That which shares the life of God, With Him surviveth all.' " MB 150

"The Holy Spirit, which proceeds from the only-begotten Son of God, binds the human agent, body, soul, and spirit, to the perfect, divine-human nature of Christ." 1SM 251

"Christ gives them the breath of His own spirit, the life of His own life." DA 827

"Eat of His flesh, drink of His blood, and you will become one with the Father and with the Son." DA 390

"This is the reception of the Holy Spirit, to know God and Jesus

111

Christ whom he has sent." 6MR 57

"After the Saviour's ascension, the sense of the divine presence, full of love and light, was still with them. It was a personal presence.... The light and love and power of an indwelling Christ shone out through them, so that men, beholding, marveled." AA 65

The Father, the Son, and the Holy Spirit

"Go ye therefore, and teach all nations, baptizing them in the name of the Father, and of the Son, and of the Holy Ghost." Matthew 28:19

"They are baptized in the name of the Father and the Son and the Holy Spirit. Thus they are united with the three great powers of heaven." Ev 307

"We are to co-operate with the three highest powers in heaven,—the Father, the Son, and the Holy Ghost." Ev 617

"The eternal heavenly dignitaries—God, and Christ, and the Holy Spirit—...would advance with them." Ev 616

"The Father is all the fullness of the Godhead bodily, and is invisible to mortal sight. The Son is all the fullness of the Godhead mani-fested. The Word of God declares Him to be 'the express image of His person.' 'God so loved the world, that He gave His only-begotten Son, that whosoever believeth in Him should not perish, but have everlasting life.' Here is shown the personality of the Father. The Comforter that Christ promised to send after He ascended to heaven, is the Spirit in all the fullness of the Godhead, making manifest the power of divine grace to all who receive and believe in Christ as a personal Saviour. There are three living persons of the heavenly trio; in the name of these three great powers—the Father, the Son, and the Holy Spirit—those who receive Christ by living faith are baptized, and these powers will co-operate with the obedient subjects of heaven in their efforts to live the new life in Christ." Ev 614, 615

"They have one God and one Saviour; and one Spirit—the Spirit of Christ—is to bring unity into their ranks." 9T 189